Project Management
for Small Projects

Project Management
for Small Projects

Sandra F. Rowe

///
MANAGEMENTCONCEPTS

ſſſ MANAGEMENTCONCEPTS

8230 Leesburg Pike, Suite 800
Vienna, VA 22182
(703) 790-9595
Fax: (703) 790-1371
www.managementconcepts.com

Printed in the United States of America

Library of Congress Cataloging-in-Publication Data

Rowe, Sandra F. (Sandra Faye), 1961–
   Project management for small projects / Sandra F. Rowe.
     p. cm.
   Includes bibliographical references and index.
   ISBN 1-56726-185-X
    1. Project management. I. Title.

HD69.P75R69 2007
658.4'04—dc22

2006046825

Character First!

Character First! definitions and information used by permission. Copyright Character Training Institute *www.characterfirst.com*

Project Management Institute

Project Management Institute, *A Guide to the Project Management Body of Knowledge (PMBOK® Guide)—Third Edition*, Project Management Institute, Inc., 2004. Copyright and all rights reserved. Material from this publication has been reproduced with the permission of PMI.

About the Author

Sandra F. Rowe, PMP, MBA, MSCIS, has more than 20 years of project management experience. Her responsibilities have included leading information technology and process improvement projects; developing project management processes, tools, and techniques; and designing, developing, and delivering project management training programs. She also has taught graduate level project management courses.

Sandra speaks regularly at project management conferences on a variety of topics related to project management processes, project management for small projects, and the project office.

Sandra is a member of PMI® and received her PMP in 1995. Her educational background includes a bachelor's of science in business, a master's of business administration, and a master's of science in computer and information systems. Sandra welcomes email at sandrarowe@comcast.net.

Dedication

Thanks to Karen Maher, Barbara Nagrant,
Sylvia Graham, and Mary Joan Tully
for being excellent project management
role models.

Special thanks to Donna Lynn Waller for
your support and your willingness to
share your project management expertise.

Contents

for larger projects and tailor them for small projects, while staying true to PMI's project management standards.

Sandra F. Rowe
Southfield, Michigan

Project Management Discipline

managed proactively, regardless of size. Normally when we think of projects, we think of large initiatives such as developing a new product or service, developing a new information system or enhancing an existing one, constructing a building, or preparing for a major sports event. Small projects are not always viewed as projects and therefore are not always treated as projects—especially smaller, more informal projects, which are often called assignments.

Definition of a Project

As stated in the *PMBOK® Guide*, Third Edition, a *project* is a temporary endeavor undertaken to create a unique product or service. A project has three distinct characteristics.

1. *A project is temporary* in that it has a beginning and an end. A project always has a defined start and end date. The project begins with a statement of work or some form of description of the product or service to be supplied by the project, and it ends when the objectives are complete or it is determined that the objectives cannot be met and the project is canceled.
2. *A project is unique* in that products, services, or results are created as a result of the project. *Unique* also indicates that although a project might appear to be similar to another project because you are producing the same type of deliverable, it really is not. In both projects you are creating something that did not exist before. Even a revision to an existing deliverable is considered unique because the revised product is something that did not exist before.
3. *A project is characterized by progressive elaboration.* This means the project develops in steps and grows in detail. Progressive elaboration is continually improving and detailing a plan as more detailed and specific information and more accurate estimates become available as the project progresses. When you are first given a project, you have limited information to work with, usually in the form of a high-level project description, the project objective, and some assumptions and constraints. The scope might need to be further defined, and the work ac-

tivities for the project need will have to be planned in detail as more specific information becomes available.

Another way to view a project is to see a project as something we do one time, as opposed to operational work, which is continuous and repetitive and is undertaken to sustain the business. Operational activities have no real completion date. An example of a project would be to develop or enhance an accounting system. The operational activity would be to process biweekly payroll or pay monthly expenses.

Why Use Project Management on Small Projects	Imagine being assigned a project to revise an existing process. You have a team of three subject matter experts to assist with the design and implementation. Where do you begin? What are you planning to deliver? When will this project be completed? And what are the team members' roles and responsibilities? The use of project management provides the discipline and tools for answering these questions.

Definition of a Small Project

All small projects are perceived to be relatively easy, but other than this there is no one way to define when a project is a small project. In some cases *small* could be defined on the basis of cost, such as costing less than $1 million. Cost is relative, however, and depends on the income of the organization. *Small* could also be defined by time, for example, taking less than six months to complete. For the purpose of this book, we will use the following guidelines to define small projects. A small project generally:

- Is short in duration, typically lasting less than six months, and usually part-time in effort hours
- Has 10 or fewer team members
- Involves a small number of skill areas
- Has a single objective and a solution that is readily achievable
- Has a narrowly defined scope and definition
- Affects a single business unit and has a single decision maker

- Has access to project information and will not require automated solutions from external project sources
- Uses the project manager as the primary source for leadership and decision-making
- Has no political implications with respect to proceeding or not proceeding
- Produces straightforward deliverables with few interdependencies among skill areas
- Costs less than $75,000 and has available funding

If the project involves a few skill areas but the deliverables are complex, it is not a small project. If the scope is broad, the project usually involves more skill areas, so it would not be considered a small project. The more skill areas involved, the more effort will be required to manage the project.

A small project can be a portion of a larger project. For example, if a team lead is responsible for planning and controlling specific project activities and then reporting results to the project manager, the team lead is, in effect, running a small project. Most small projects center on changes in organizational processes. Other examples of small projects include:

- Developing a training course
- Implementing a project office
- Implementing a purchased software application
- Enhancing an existing information system
- Developing a website
- Evaluating an existing practice
- Developing a strategy
- Developing a project proposal

The following are detailed descriptions of two small projects.

Develop a Training Course on Introduction to Project Management

Characteristics	Criteria
Duration	Six months
Team members	Five part-time team members: project manager, instructional designer, two trainers, and an administrative assistant
Single objective	Develop Introduction to Project Management training course
Narrowly defined scope	Training materials in alignment with other project management courses
Single decision-maker	Sponsor: corporate education director
Straightforward deliverables	PowerPoint presentation, facilitator's manual, participant's manual, and case study
Interdependencies among skill areas	Project Management Office

Revise the Current Project Management Planning Process

Characteristics	Criteria
Duration	Three months
Team members	Four part-time team members: project manager and three subject matter experts
Single objective	Revise the planning process to include changes made to the corporate project management process and to be consistent with the current *PMBOK*®
Narrowly defined scope	Planning process description and templates
Single decision-maker	Sponsor: Project Office director
Straightforward deliverables	Planning process description, work breakdown structure process and example, brainstorming techniques, project-planning templates
Interdependencies among skill areas	None

Definition of a Simple Project

This book differentiates between small and simple projects. Many of the best practices for small projects and simple projects are similar. When small projects and simple projects require different approaches, this book explains where and how.

Simple projects are even more straightforward than small projects. Simple projects are often called assignments. We usually do not think of assignments as projects, but assignments, like projects, have a definite beginning and end and produce a unique output. Assignments are usually short in duration and are completed by a small team consisting of three or fewer team members. Often only one person completes an assignment. Refer to Chapter 13, The Power of One, for more details on one-person assignments.

Because we do not think of assignments as projects, we do not treat them as projects. Assignments, because of their size and duration, do not need all the formality required by projects; however, they can still benefit from a simplified form of project management. Treating assignments as projects provides you with the opportunity to clearly define expectations, better use resources, and eliminate the frustration of wasted effort and unnecessary rework.

Examples of simple projects include:

- Developing procedures or a reference guide
- Revising a business process
- Developing an electronic filing system to store departmental documents
- Developing a presentation to communicate a new process

The factors that distinguish a small project from a simple project are duration, team size, and degree of formality required to effectively meet stakeholders' expectations. The project manager must determine what combination of processes and tools fits the needs of the project.

WHAT IS PROJECT MANAGEMENT?

Project management is the application of knowledge, skills, tools, and techniques to meet project requirements. It includes defining and planning the necessary work, scheduling the activities to complete the work, monitoring and controlling project activities, and finally conducting activities to end the project.

Project management involves coordinating the work of other people. A project manager and a project team are involved in the project. The project manager is the person assigned by the organization to achieve the project objectives. *Project manager* might not be the person's formal job title, but for the purpose of this book we will use the term for the person responsible for completing the project. The project team members are the people responsible for performing project work. They complete the project deliverables. They might or might not report directly to the project manager. For small projects team members usually work part-time on the project.

Is project management an art or science? It is both.

Project management is an art because the project manager must use management and leadership skills that are applied on the basis of the project situation and are unique to each project. Some of these skills are communicating, negotiating, decision-making, and problem-solving. The art of project management requires the project manager to gain agreement between technical and business resources, the project team and the customer, and multiple stakeholders. (*Stakeholders* are people and organizations that are actively involved in the project or whose interests might be positively or negatively affected as a result of project execution or project completion.) To effectively master the art of project management, you must have a degree of proficiency with the science of project management.

Project management is a science because it is based on repeatable processes and techniques. The project manager has an array of tools, templates, and standards to assist with planning a project. In addition, the project manager has an assortment of metrics and status reports for monitoring and controlling a project. Mastering the science of project management is dependent on the effectiveness and efficiency of applying the appropriate project management processes and techniques.

It's been said that project managers spend about 75 to 80 percent of their time on the art of project management and 20 to 25 percent of their time on the science.

The Power of Project Management   A team was assigned to work on a project to revise an existing system. Since the changes were minor and the project was only expected to last five weeks, the project manager was lax in the use of project management processes and tools. Needless to say, the project got into trouble. The project work was not completed on time and the team was discouraged. A new project manager was assigned who insisted on the use of project management best practices. A project charter was developed that gave the team a clear understanding of what was included in the project. The team then worked together to develop the project schedule, which included the name of the resource responsible for completing the work along with the planned start and end dates. The team became reenergized and engaged in completing the project activities.

VALUE OF USING PROJECT MANAGEMENT ON SMALL PROJECTS

Project success can be defined as on time, within budget, and meeting the requirements of the project stakeholders. Managers of small projects need to be concerned with meeting this triple constraint.

The value project management offers is the use of standard processes and tools. Project management is even more valuable when the processes and tools can be tailored to fit the different types and sizes of small projects. By using a methodology, the project manager is more prepared to define and manage the project scope, obtain project requirements, and provide ongoing communications. Stakeholders are engaged early and expectations are known. Add to this the ability to produce realistic estimates and schedules, and to effectively manage issues and risks, and you have a means of managing the triple constraints. When you can manage the triple constraints, you improve your chances for project success.

Finally, using project management on small projects will provide models for future projects. Most small projects tend to be similar in structure or outcome. If a template or model is developed, it can be used for future projects. This saves the project manager time and provides a basis for continuous process improvement.

Why Use Project Management?

Project management:

- Provides processes and tools that create discipline and a means for organizing project data
- Provides a means to define scope and control scope changes
- Defines project roles and responsibilities
- Allows the project manager to manage stakeholder expectations
- Allows the team to focus on priorities
- Manages the triple constraints: time, cost, and requirements

---

2

Concerns for Small Projects

We have determined that a project is a series of activities that must be performed to achieve a specific goal, within a specific timeframe, and that small projects require a degree of discipline to be successful. Now we look at the challenges and problems associated with managing small projects.

CHALLENGES FOR SMALL PROJECTS

A challenge is a call to action. Some challenges the project manager should respond to are identified below.

Planning

Planning is necessary to define and mature the project scope, develop the project management plan, and identify and schedule the project activities that occur within the project. Planning is a challenge for a project of any size. Getting the right people together at the right time to discuss the project details can be painful.

Planning for a small project is even more of a challenge. The project is already perceived as being easy to deliver because of its size. Small equals easy. Because of that perception, adequate time is not set aside for detailed planning. (Why waste time planning when you could be creating project deliverables?) The first reaction after receiving the small project is to jump right in and start performing the project activities without planning. Even the most experienced project manager has fallen into this trap at least once. By not planning, you start out thinking the project is small and then end up hoping that the project really is small. Also, by not planning you may overlook a critical component of the project.

The project manager should always make sure the scope, work effort, and costs are defined. With a loosely defined scope, the project manager runs the risk of it constantly changing, and scope creep could become a problem. The project manager should also make time to plan because the plan provides direction for the project and is a communication tool for the sponsor and other project stakeholders. Planning gives the project the respect it deserves.

When planning a small project, the project manager should consider a few things.

- **Remember to plan.** It is easy to overlook the importance of planning on a small project. Add the planning deliverables to your list of project deliverables.
- **Involve the people who will do the work in planning the work.** It is easy for you to quickly create a plan based on what should be done, but the people who will do the work have more accurate information on what really needs to be done, how much effort it will actually take, and when they are available to do the work. Without this information, even a small project will fail.
- **Be careful not to overplan or become too detailed.** Decide how much detail is required and know when enough is enough.
- **Control the urge to structure the project in a way that overemphasizes the elements you are most comfortable with.** The result of this can be that you don't give the attention required to the elements with which you are not as comfortable. Remember: Don't get stuck on what you know.

Planning activities for small and simple projects might be time-consuming initially, but in the long term planning will save time and effort and reduce the risk of failure. Remember that even on a small project you should not work in a vacuum. Obtain input from stakeholders, and schedule project reviews with the project sponsor.

Project Challenge: Planning	Because small projects are generally short in duration and are perceived as easy to deliver, planning is often omitted as the team immediately begins working on producing project deliverables. Without the exercise of defining all of the deliverables and estimating the effort required to complete the deliverables, this team has already unknowingly put the project in jeopardy.

A team of three was assigned to develop a training course. Because the team members were all trainers, they were confident that they could develop a training course with no problem. They separated the course into six modules, and each trainer took two and immediately began developing presentation slides for the course. A week later the sponsor asked for an update and was told by the team that the project was on schedule and that the course would be developed in four weeks. Still operating with no defined deliverables, no schedule, no roles and responsibilities, no criteria for success, and no communication methods, the team members continued to independently design presentation slides.

With two days left the team met to review its progress. Each trainer had developed two modules based on their own design. Since the deliverables were not defined, some of the modules were detailed and included activities and some were general and just included basic definitions. The responses were, "Oh, I didn't know you wanted to include that," or "Oh, that's a good idea. Why didn't you tell me what you were doing? What are we going to do now?" But with two days left, how was the team going to deliver a quality product to the sponsor? The team did what many teams do when they know they are going to miss a deadline: it asked the sponsor for more time.

The team had to explain to the sponsor why it was not able to make the deadline. This was embarrassing for the team, because, after all, this was a small project (remember the perception—easy to deliver). The sponsor asked the team how much more time it needed. Before responding, this time the team did some planning. It defined the deliverables, estimated the effort, and established ongoing communication vehicles. To fail once was bad enough. The team members had learned their lesson. They understood now that even for a small project, if they wanted to be successful, they had to plan their project activities.

Reasons **to Plan**	Here is a summary of the reasons you should always plan: • Scope, work effort, and costs are defined • The plan is a communication tool for project stakeholders • The plan provides the means to control the project • The plan increases the opportunity for project success

Low Prioritization

Another challenge for managing small projects is that the projects often have low priority within the organization. The project has low visibility and is often less important than larger projects, and is therefore treated as a lower priority in the daily activities of the project team members. The project manager must work hard to convey a sense of project urgency.

The project manager can increase the importance of a low priority project in the eyes of the project team by helping the team see how the project fits into the organization. This line of sight connects the team member with the small project, strategic initiative, organizational goal, and finally all the way up to the company vision. Connecting the small project to the organization's goals gives the project a stronger identity and the team members an understanding that they are part of something larger than "just" the small project.

Inexperienced Project Teams

Small projects rarely have a dedicated project team and have difficulty obtaining key resources. Often a small project is staffed with inexperienced or less-skilled team members because the small project is viewed as not requiring the more highly skilled resources.

A small project might be given to an inexperienced project manager to provide an opportunity for the project manager to develop project management skills. Without the benefit of prior training or mentoring, such project managers are often left to their own devices or might not know what to do.

Having an inexperienced project team should not discourage the project manager. Many times, less experienced project team members are eager to learn and often request the opportunity to be part of the team. If people want to learn, they are more willing to try new things. Having an inexperienced team is also an opportunity for the project manager to build an informal network, as everyone on the team, including the project manager, learns together.

Project Manager Responsible for Multiple Functions

The project manager might have to perform multiple functions and could sacrifice project management for the sake of getting the work done. In addition to managing the project, the project manager might be involved in one or more of the following:

- **Operating as the subject matter expert on a given project.** As the subject matter expert, the project manager might take on the role of the analyst, specialist, designer, or developer, to name a few. As the subject matter expert, the project manager might be responsible for performing analyses, gathering business requirements, developing specifications, creating deliverables, or testing or implementing deliverables. To state it another way, the project manager might perform the tasks required to complete the project.
- **Being responsible for operational activities.** The project manager might manage projects part-time and also have ongoing operational responsibilities.
- **Managing more than one project.** With small projects, there is a greater chance that the project manager will be assigned to more than one. (Refer to Chapter 11 for additional information on managing multiple projects.)

Process and Tools

Using the right processes and tools is a challenge because in many cases they are not available for small projects. In addition, it is a mistake to assume that if the process and tools work for large projects, they can be applied to small projects without modification.

Trying to fit a small project into the process and tools designed for a large project will not work. Using more process than required is time-consuming and frustrating. Small projects need a short turnaround time. If plans cannot be produced quickly and key information cannot be communicated rapidly, the project is hurt. With a short timeframe, there is no time for rework. What usually happens is that the project manager moves forward without thoroughly planning the work and quickly loses control.

PROBLEMS FROM NOT USING PROJECT MANAGEMENT

Sometimes project managers choose to omit project management techniques. When this happens, the project manager is open to some possible problems—project failure, project manager failure, or both.

Project Failure

Many of the problems that occur from not using project management on large projects also occur on small projects—for example, scope creep, conflicting priorities, and unclear goals. These problems often lead to project failure, where the project results are not delivered as expected. Project failure usually means the project is delivered late, has a cost overrun, does not meet the requirements, or any combination of the three.

Factors that contribute to the failure of a small project include:

- Insufficient or inadequate resources
- Insufficient planning and control

- Lack of current project documentation, especially plans, status reports, and risk logs
- Unrealistic schedules
- Lack of participation from project sponsor
- Lack of participation from project team (project team members do not participate in key decisions or assume responsibility for their project activities)
- Inexperienced project manager

At times, small projects fail because we lose focus on what we are supposed to accomplish or produce. We get distracted by other projects or priorities and when we are able to return to the small project, it takes time to remember where we left off and even more time to get back on track.

Project Failure A project is usually considered a failure if it is late, over budget, or does not meet the customer's expectations. Without the control that project management provides, a project is more likely to have problems with one of these areas. A problem with only one constraint (time, cost, or requirements) can jeopardize the entire project.

Project Manager Failure

A problem unique to small projects is related to the project manager's reputation. A project manager's reputation suffers if he or she does not manage a small project successfully. The perception is that small projects are easier to manage, and therefore the expectation is always to have 100 percent success. Because small projects are viewed as easier to manage, they are sometimes used as a training ground to prepare a project manager for larger projects. A project manager who is unsuccessful in managing a small project runs the risk of professional embarrassment and possible career advancement delays.

Using project management on small projects allows the project manager to develop project management competency. The project manager will first acquire knowledge—an understanding of project management theory, processes, and practice. Then the project manager will develop skills at a level of proficiency needed to carry out project responsibilities. Small projects really are a training ground or an opportunity to prove that you are ready for something bigger.

| **What Happens if a Project Manager Fails** | When project managers fail on a large project, they might get a second chance by being reassigned to a small project. When project managers fail on a small project, what's left? The moral: Use project management tools to maximize your chance of success! |

3

Managing and Leading Small Projects

The project manager is responsible for the overall success of the project. To be successful, the project manager must both manage and lead the small project. It has often been said that managers do things right and leaders do the right things. This combination of effectiveness and efficiency is what makes a good project manager. This chapter provides more specifics on what it means to both manage and lead small projects.

MANAGING SMALL PROJECTS

To *manage* is to have charge of or responsibility for the project. Management includes general management knowledge and skills and project management knowledge and skills. In general, the project manager plans, organizes, directs, and controls project activities. More specifically, for small projects the project manager manages project resources, focuses on the project timeline, and documents project activities.

The best way to view project management practices is through the *PMBOK® Guide*'s Project Management Knowledge Areas. Project Management Knowledge Areas are areas of project management that are defined by knowledge requirements and described in terms of their component processes, practices, inputs, outputs, tools, and techniques. PMI has identified nine Project Management Knowledge Areas for use in managing projects. This section builds off the *PMBOK® Guide*, Third Edition, definitions for each knowledge area and describes how each knowledge area can be applied to small projects.

dissemination, storage, and ultimate disposition of project information. Project Communication Management activities include communications planning, information distribution, performance reporting, and stakeholder management. For small projects, these activities can be accomplished by:
  – Developing a communications matrix
  – Producing status reports
  – Managing stakeholder expectations
- *Project Risk Management* describes the processes concerned with conducting risk management on a project. Project Risk Management activities include risk management planning, risk identification, qualitative risk analysis, quantitative risk analysis, risk response planning, and risk monitoring and control. For small projects, these activities can be accomplished by:
  – Defining how risks will be managed
  – Identifying project risks
  – Analyzing project risks
  – Developing a risk register
  – Tracking identified risks and identifying new risks as the project progresses
- *Project Procurement Management* describes the processes that purchase or acquire products, services, or results, as well as contract management processes. Project Procurement Management includes activities to plan purchases and acquisitions, plan contracting, requesting seller responses, selecting a seller, contract administration, and contract closure. Project Procurement Management activities are not included in the methodology for small projects included in this book.

Although the Project Management Knowledge Areas are applicable to small projects, not all of them have to be used in their entirety or on every small project. They are included in this book because in order to become an expert manager of small projects, the project manager must understand the knowledge areas and know which ones are applicable for the small project and which ones can be omitted. This is a project-by-project decision.

At first glance, these management activities may appear to be overwhelming and too much process for a small project. But don't worry—these activities are explained in more detail in the project management process section, which provides tips and tools for scaling the project management activities to fit the needs of the project.

LEADING SMALL PROJECTS

To *lead* is to go before or with and show others the way. It is to guide in direction, course, action, and opinion. A good leader has the ability to motivate others to accomplish an objective. Being a leader is not about having a title; it is about having followers. People will follow you because they have to or because they want to. In reality, most project managers of small projects have to lead based on influence, not authority. Having the ability to lead, even on a small project, will enhance your project management success. Remember that leading is the art of project management.

As a leader the project manager should develop and sell the project vision, set the direction and pace of the project, coach and empower the project team, facilitate communication with all project stakeholders, and demonstrate good character. A lot of material regarding the importance of leadership skills is available; however, the importance of good character is worth mentioning.

Character defines the person. Character First! defines *character* as the qualities built into a person's life that determine his or her response, regardless of circumstances. (Character First! was developed in 1991 by Tom Hill and assists with the development of good character by defining 49 character qualities). Character is the inward motivation to do what is right in every situation. An effective leader has good character. Character development takes place every day. To continuously build character, the project manager should emphasize the importance of good character. The project manager should never accept bad behavior from team members and should always recognize and praise team members for displaying good character.

Building off Character First!, here are some character qualities that are important in leadership:

- **Availability**—Making your schedule and priorities secondary to the needs of the project team
- **Compassion**—Investing whatever is necessary to heal the hurts of project stakeholders
- **Creativity**—Approaching a need, a task, or an idea from a new perspective
- **Decisiveness**—Having the ability to recognize key factors and finalize difficult decisions
- **Determination**—Intending to accomplish project goals at the right time, regardless of the opposition
- **Diligence**—Investing time and energy to complete the project
- **Flexibility**—Being willing to change plans or ideas according to the direction of key project stakeholders
- **Forgiveness**—Clearing the record of those who have wronged you and not holding a grudge
- **Integrity**—Adhering to moral and ethical principles
- **Orderliness**—Arranging yourself and your surroundings to achieve greater efficiency
- **Patience**—Accepting a difficult situation without giving a deadline to remove it
- **Respect**—Showing regard or consideration for a person or position
- **Responsibility**—Knowing and doing what is expected
- **Self-control**—Rejecting wrong desires and doing what is right
- **Tolerance**—Realizing that others are at varying levels of character development
- **Truthfulness**—Earning future trust by accurately reporting past facts
- **Wisdom**—Seeing and responding to project situations from a perspective that transcends your current situation

This is not an all-inclusive list of character traits; it merely highlights some important leadership traits that can be developed over time.

MANAGING VERSUS LEADING A PROJECT

You should *manage* processes and *lead* people.

- Managing requires that the project manager plan, organize, direct, and control project activities by developing plans and keeping them current, understanding the needs of the project stakeholders and responding appropriately, resolving issues, and producing status reports. These are the routine activities that are essential for success.

- Leading requires interaction with people. The project manager must command authority and be able to inspire and motivate others. The project manager sets the general direction of the project and allows team members to provide input along the way. During difficult times, the project manager must remain calm and be able to provide solutions to get things back on track.

In order to effectively manage and lead, the project manager must have communication, facilitation, problem-solving and decision-making skills.

Good and Poor Project Managers	A good project manager listens to the team, allows the team members to perform project activities, makes decisions in a timely manner, and rewards the team for success.
	A poor project manager is only concerned for him- or herself, does not respond to the needs of the team, blames the team when things go wrong, and takes all the credit when the team is successful.

MANAGING AND LEADING SIMPLE PROJECTS

Simple projects require both management and leadership; however, the time spent on these activities and how the activities are performed are based on the amount of work required for completing the project. The project manager should always understand the project objective, define the project scope, plan project activities, manage project resources, and communicate with key stakeholders. Short-duration projects just require less formality.

4

Pre-Project Activities

The project management process that is discussed in Chapter 5 begins after the project has been defined and approved. But how does a project get started? If you have an idea for a project and need to document your idea in order to get it approved, the project request is an excellent tool. If you have the opportunity to determine what could be worked on as a project, you should also use the project request.

The purpose of the project request is to identify the business need and outline the potential project. The person or area that is trying to get a project approved completes the project request. The project request is then submitted to the decision-maker or approval committee.

The decision-maker will determine whether or not to proceed with the project. In addition to approving the project, the decision-maker may also give the project a priority and indicate when the project can begin.

The project request consists of the following:

- **Business Information**
  - *Business Area*—Identify the organization or department requesting the project.
  - *Business Need or Opportunity*—Identify why this project is important and how it supports the business goal(s).
  - *Link to Strategic Objective*—Identify the strategic objective this project supports.
  - *Customer*—Identify the end user of the project.

- **Project Description**
  - *Objective*—State what the project will achieve. The project objectives support the business need or opportunity. Objectives should be SMART—specific, measurable, attainable/achievable, realistic, and time-bound.
  - *Scope*—Identify what is included in the project.
  - *Desired Completion Date*—Provide a high-level estimate of when you expect the project to be completed.
  - *Preliminary Funding Estimate*—Provide a high-level estimate of what the project will cost.
- **Project Information**
  - *Assumptions*—Assumptions are the factors that, for planning purposes, are considered true, real, or certain. Assumptions are events or conditions that must occur for the project to be successful, but at this time they are not certain. Clearly and concisely state the assumptions so everyone knows the premises on which the project request is based.
  - *Issues*—Identify points or matters that are in question or in dispute or a point or matter that is not settled and is under discussion or about which there are opposing views or disagreements.
  - *Risks*—Identify any uncertain event or condition that, if it occurs, will have a positive or negative effect on the project's objectives.
  - *Acceptance Criteria*—Explain how you will know the project is considered complete and successful.

Project Request Example

Jackson Project Management Group is a consulting firm that offers a variety of project management services. Faye Jackson, founder and president, insists that her organization use project management best practices. One of the strategic goals for this year is to offer project management training. Faye asked Mary, the director of the newly established training organization, to provide a list of potential project management courses, along with the course description.

Mary developed a list of ten potential courses. Two were introductory or beginning level, three were intermediate level, and five were advanced level.

Faye was impressed with the course descriptions and decided to start with one of the beginning level courses, a course called Project Management Overview. She would like to deliver the first course the third quarter of this year. Faye asked Mary to sponsor the development of the course and to develop the project request, which is shown in Figure 4.1.

Project Request

Request Date	Project Name		
1/21/XX	Project Management Overview Course		
Project Sponsor	Contact Name		Project Type
Mary	Mary		

Business Information

Business Area
Project Management Training Department
Business Need
To develop a beginning level project management training course to offer to the general public.
Link to Strategic Objective
Offer project management training courses.
Customer
Training department

Project Description

Objective
Develop a beginning level project management course that can be offered to the general public beginning third quarter 20XX.
Scope
The project scope includes: classroom training materials for the facilitator and participants. Web-based training solutions are not included in this project.
Desired Completion Date
5/31/XX
Preliminary Funding Estimate
$100,000

Project Information

Assumptions
No outside resources will be required to develop the course materials.
Issues
None at this time.
Risks
None at this time.
Acceptance Criteria
Course materials are approved by the pilot team.

FIGURE 4.1   Project Request

Project Management Process for Small Projects

5

Process Overview

A project management methodology provides the structure and discipline for managing projects. Using such a methodology increases your odds of project success. To more effectively manage small projects, a methodology specifically designed for small projects should be used. The Small and Simple Project Management (SSPM) methodology, which is an invention of the author of this book and is the method presented in this book, provides the framework, processes, tools, and techniques to manage small projects, and it can be further tailored for simple projects.

In addition to a project management methodology, projects will also need a defined project life cycle methodology. Together, the project management methodology and project life cycle methodology provide the structure for bringing a project to completion.

Advantages of Small and Simple Project Management Methodology	The Small and Simple Project Management methodology: • Was developed out of necessity, because methodologies for large projects were too cumbersome for small and simple projects • Was designed specifically for small projects • Contains easy-to-use templates • Provides step-by-step procedures • Contains process guides for easy reference

---

PROJECT LIFE CYCLE

The *PMBOK® Guide*, Third Edition, defines a *project life cycle* as a collection of generally sequential project phases whose name and number are determined by the control needs of the organization or organizations involved in the project. The project life cycle represents a specific industry, product, or service and defines the phases of a project from beginning to end. For example, a project life cycle to enhance an existing software application includes definition, requirements, analysis, design, construction, testing, implementation, and post-implementation.

Phases provide management control because each phase defines the work that should occur and results in a deliverable or deliverables that are passed on to the next phase. More specifically, a project life cycle defines the technical work required for each phase, when the deliverables are to be generated, who is involved, and how to control the work. It also provides review points for the project so that go/no go decisions can be made.

Other Project Life Cycles   Other project life cycles or project methodologies include:

- Instructional design process
- Web design
- Process improvement
- Project outsourcing

A generic project life cycle for small projects, shown in Figure 5.1, includes

- Requirements definition
- Design
- Development
- Testing
- Implementation
- Post-implementation review

These phases are usually short, and some may be combined or planned at the phase level. Refer to the planning chapters (Chapters 7 and 8) for more details.

It is important for the project manager to understand the project life cycle because the project life cycle defines what the project will

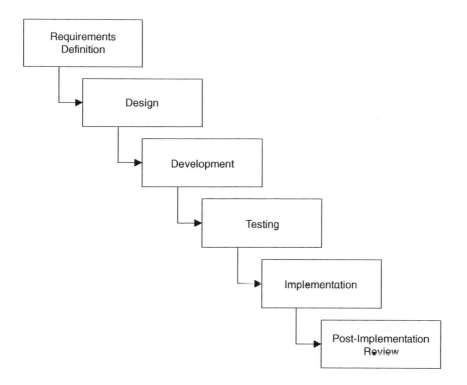

FIGURE 5.1   Generic Project Life Cycle for Small Projects

deliver. A generic project life cycle can be used for most small projects because most small projects are not industry specific and do
not require a specific methodology. If a small project has a defined
methodology, that methodology should be used. Specific details related to project life cycle or product deliverables are not discussed
in this book because the content varies from project to project. The
project management of the project life cycle or product deliverables
remains constant. The focus of this book is on how to produce standard project management deliverables.

DELIVERABLES

The *PMBOK® Guide*, Third Edition, defines a *deliverable* as any
unique and verifiable product, result, or capability to perform a ser-

vice that must be produced to complete a process, phase, or project. There are two types of deliverables: final and interim. Final deliverables are delivered to the customer, and interim deliverables are produced as part of the process of creating the final deliverable. For example, a project might require a procedure manual as the final deliverable. The individual sections or drafts of the procedure manual are the interim deliverables.

Most small projects can be managed using deliverables. The project manager can plan and control project progress for deliverables at the task level, which is how most project are normally managed. Tasks can be added for specificity only if the additional details improve the project manager's ability to monitor and control the project activities. Otherwise, the use of only deliverables and interim deliverables allows the project manager to scale the process and tools to fit the project's needs. Managing using deliverables is covered in more detail in Chapters 7 and 8.

PROJECT MANAGEMENT PROCESS FOR SMALL PROJECTS

Effective project management is based on a repeatable process for describing, organizing, and completing the work of the project. Small projects can be effectively managed; although they do not require as much formality as large projects, some form of project management discipline is suggested. What is needed is a process specifically designed for small projects. Applying a process designed for a large project to a small project could prove to be worse than not using a process.

SSPM Process Overview

A *process* is a set of interrelated actions and activities that are performed to achieve a pre-specified set of products, results, or services. The SSPM process is specifically designed for small projects and can be adjusted for simple projects and assignments. A good process is consistent and can be applied to all projects.

It is important to note that for a process to be effective for small projects, it must be both scalable and adaptable. It should be scalable so that the level of complexity of the project management process, the time spent in using the process, and the focus of the process all fit the needs of the project. It should be adaptable so that the tools chosen to support the project can be easily applied. The tools are flexible, but the process does not change.

Another aspect of the SSPM process is that the emphasis is placed on deliverables, with a focus on templates and checklists. Process guides keep the process visible and easy to follow. You can find process guides in Chapters 6–10.

Project Management Process Description

The SSPM process defines the overall project management life cycle and the phases by which to organize the project. It explains how to move among project management phases within the project, how to determine specific assignments to do the work, and what action is taken to complete the work. Some methodologies refer to the process groupings as *stages*, *chunks*, or *steps*. We use the term *phase* to represent a specific collection of project management activities.

The following is a summary of the SSPM process. Each phase will be explained in detail in the following chapters. The four project management phases are:

1. **Initiating Process**—Includes the activities conducted to start up the project. The initiating process defines and authorizes the project. (See Chapter 6.)
2. **Planning Process**—Includes the activities to define the project in detail and determines how the project objectives will be achieved. (See Chapters 7 and 8.)
3. **Controlling Process**—Include the activities to carry out the project activities, measure and monitor progress, and take corrective action when necessary. (See Chapter 9.)
4. **Closing Process**—Includes the activities to bring the project to an end. (See Chapter 10.)

The SSPM process is consistent with *PMBOK®* except that the phases execute, monitor, and control have been combined for simplicity. Figure 5-2 shows the SSPM process.

PMBOK® is very important in the world of project management and has set the standard for good practices, so it is important to know how the SSPM process differs form the *PMBOK®* process groups. Also, as you prepare to make the transition from smaller to larger projects, more process will be required.

The *PMBOK®* process groups are:

- **Initiating Process Group**—Defines and authorizes the project or a project phase
- **Planning Process Group**—Defines and refines objectives, and plans the course of action required to attain the objectives and scope that the project was undertaken to address
- **Executing Process Group**—Integrates people and other resources to carry out the project management plan for the project
- **Monitoring and Controlling Process Group**—Regularly measures and monitors progress to identify variances from the project management plan so that corrective action can be taken when necessary to meet project objectives
- **Closing Process Group**—Formalizes acceptance of the product, service, or result and brings the project or project phase to an orderly end

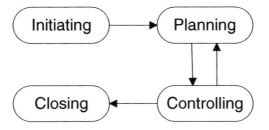

FIGURE 5.2   Small and Simple Project Management Process

It is important to distinguish between the project life cycle and the project management process. The project life cycle is linear and defines the deliverables for each phase, whereas the project management process occurs for each phase, can recur multiple times within a phase, and is used to define the actions for completing the work. The project life cycle and the project management process, although separate and distinct, are integrated to allow the project manager to manage the entire project from start to finish.

PALM PRINCIPLE

The SSPM process previously discussed is designed for small projects; however, at times it will be too much process for your immediate project needs. The PALM principle (Figure 5.3) is a component of the SSPM process and is used for simple projects—projects that do not need much project management formality. Any of the SSPM process documents can be used as needed to support PALM.

The PALM principle includes the following:

- *Plan* project activities. Always take time to think through what needs to be accomplished, who is involved, and the timeframe for completing the work.

Plan project activities
Analyze the situation and ask questions
Lead the project activities
Monitor and control time and resources

FIGURE 5.3 PALM Principle

- *Analyze* the situation and ask questions. Use project management tools as needed to make good decisions.
- *Lead* the project activities. Initiate communication with stakeholders. Make sure your project gets the attention it deserves.
- *Monitor and control* time and resources.

The PALM principle requires minimal documentation. The focus is on behavior. Your attitude about how to approach a simple project will determine how other people will support your efforts.

LEADERSHIP CONNECTION

The project manager is responsible for leading the project team. Based on the previous definition of small projects, small projects typically have small teams. One of the first things the project manager must do with the project team is to communicate the processes that will be used on the project. Processes must be established at the beginning of the project and be understood by the team.

The project manager should:

- Determine how much process is required for the project and which tools are appropriate.
- Make the project management process understandable and visible.
- Understand the project life cycle for the project and integrate the life cycle and management processes as needed.
- Understand and respect project roles and responsibilities.

KEYS FOR PROCESS SUCCESS

Keys for process success include:

- Make sure the right amount of process is used for each project. If too much or too little is used initially, be flexible enough to make the necessary adjustments.
- Keep process guides handy for quick reference.

- Integrate the project management process with the product development process to gain more efficiency.
- Lead the way for other project managers to begin using project management on small projects.

6

Initiating

That the project get off to a good start is important. The initiating process allows the project manager to quickly define project objectives, scope, assumptions, constraints, and risk factors. It is also important at this time for the project manager to develop a relationship with the project sponsor and to discuss project management expectations.

For the purposes of the Small and Simple Project Management (SSPM) process, it is assumed that the decision to launch the project has already been made, the staffing has been approved, funding exists, and the project manager has been assigned. Pre-project documents like the project request, requirements overview, and project proposal have already been completed. Simple projects do not require this level of formality; as soon as the assignment is given, the initiating activities begin.

INITIATING PROCESS SUMMARY

The initiating process includes the activities conducted to start up the project.

The project manager interviews the project sponsor and stakeholders to get the information required for developing the project charter. The project charter provides structure for the project manager to use to obtain the additional information needed to plan the project. The initiation phase is meant to be quick. The project manager prepares the project charter and reviews it with the project sponsor to ensure they are both in agreement. Agreement at this point is informal, usually verbal. At the end of the initiating process, the project manager is ready to plan the project.

INITIATING PROCESS STEPS

The initiating process steps:

1. Obtain copies of pre-project documents.
2. Interview project sponsor and other stakeholders.
3. Prepare project charter.
4. Review project charter with stakeholders.
5. Obtain approval from project sponsor to begin planning.

Step 1: Obtain Copies of Pre-Project Documents

The project manager should obtain copies of all pre-project documents. These documents will differ depending on an organization's project selection and approval methodology. Many small projects are not assigned as part of a project selection methodology; they are simply given as assignments. If this is the case, the project manager should obtain any documents that supply background information for the project.

Step 2: Interview Project Sponsor and Other Stakeholders

The project sponsor shares responsibility for project success and has ultimate sign-off authority for the project. Other project stakeholders include primary customers, secondary customers, and the project team.

A key activity during the initiation phase is information gathering. The project manager must determine the stakeholders' needs and clarify their expectations. This is the time to identify what the stakeholders really want. Some ways to gather information are reviewing existing documentation, conducting interviews, distributing surveys, and observing the current operation. After the project manager has completed the information-gathering process, the information should be documented and shared with the project stakeholders.

Step 3: Prepare Project Charter

The project charter describes the project and serves as an agreement between the sponsor and the project manager. The project manager prepares this document with direction from the project sponsor. The components of the project charter are discussed in the next section.

Step 4: Review Project Charter with Stakeholders

The project manager distributes the initial draft of the project charter to key stakeholders to obtain feedback and build consensus. After the project manager receives their input, the project manager updates the project charter and distributes it to the appropriate stakeholders for buy-in.

Step 5: Obtain Approval from Project Sponsor to Begin Planning

The final initiating process step is to obtain approval from the project sponsor. After all the key project stakeholders have reviewed the project charter and provided input, the project manager shares the project charter with the project sponsor. If the project sponsor approves the project charter, the project manager can begin planning the project activities.

PROJECT CHARTER

The project manager prepares the project charter with input from the project sponsor. The purpose of the project charter is to provide the project manager with the authority to apply organizational resources to project activities. The project charter is one of the most important documents in the SSPM process because it identifies the project objectives and defines the project scope. The project charter is used as a reference throughout the project to ensure that the project scope does not change.

The deliverable from the initiating process is the project charter or an abbreviated version of the project charter, depending on the size of the project. Two versions of the project charter are covered in this chapter, the project charter and the project charter lite.

Project Charter Components

The project charter includes the following:

- **Project Roles and Responsibilities**
  - *Project Sponsor*—Identify person with ultimate responsibility for the project.
  - *Project Manager*—Identify project manager and roles and responsibilities.
  - *Other Project Stakeholders*—List other project stakeholders, including the customer or end user of the outcomes of the project.
  - *Core Team Members*—Identify key team members.
- **Project Description**
  - *Background Information*—Provide an overview of the purpose of the project and the business goals the project will support.
  - *Project Objectives*—State what the project will achieve. The project objectives define the business need or opportunity. The objectives should be SMART—specific, *m*easurable, *a*ttainable/*a*chievable, *r*ealistic, and *t*ime-bound).
  - *Project Scope*—The scope identifies the boundaries of the project by stating what will be done and what will not be done.
    - ○ *In Scope*—Identify what is included in this project.
    - ○ *Not in Scope*—Identify what is known not to be part of this project.
  - *Project Budget*—Identify the funding needed for this project.
- **Project Information**
  - *High-Level Deliverables*—List the major deliverables to be completed as part of the project.

- *Assumptions*—Assumptions are factors that for planning purposes are considered true, real, or certain. These events or conditions must occur for the project to be successful, but at this time they are not certain. Clearly and concisely state assumptions so everyone knows the premise on which the charter is based.
- *Constraints*—Constraints are restrictions that affect the performance of the project or factors that affect when an activity can be scheduled.
- *Dependencies with Other Projects*—Identify links with other projects.
- *Risks or Opportunities*—Identify uncertain events or conditions that if they occur could have a negative or positive impact on the project.
- **Supporting Information**
  - *Business Process Impact*—Note whether any existing business processes will have to change or whether new business processes will have to be developed.
  - *Acceptance Criteria*—Explain how you will know that the project is considered complete and successful.

Project Charter Example

Michael was assigned as project manager for the Project Management Overview course (from Chapter 4) and was given a copy of the project request. He met with Mary to discuss the project in more detail and used the information she provided to develop the project charter (Figure 6.1).

The Project Charter

The project charter
- Formally authorizes the project
- Documents the business needs
- Requires sponsor approval
- Is the basis for scope changes

Project Charter

Project Number	Project Name	
S107	Project Management Overview Course	
Prepared by	**Date**	**Project Type**
Michael	1/21/XX	Small

Project Description

Background Information
Jackson Project Management Group will begin offering project management training courses later this year. A training department was established to develop and deliver training courses. The Project Management Overview Course will be the first course.
Project Objectives
Develop a beginning level project management course that can be offered to the general public beginning third quarter 20XX.
Project Scope
In Scope: classroom training materials for the facilitator and participants.
Out of Scope: Web-based training solutions.
Project Budget
$100,000
Customer
Training department

Project Roles and Responsibilities

Project Sponsor
Mary Johnson
Project Manager
Michael
Other Project Stakeholders
Faye Jackson
Core Team Members
Instructional Designer, Trainer, Administrative Assistant

Project Information

High Level Deliverables
Participant's Manual, Facilitator's Manual, Presentation Slides, Case Study
Assumptions
No outside resources will be required to develop the course materials.
Constraints
Course materials must be completed in time for third quarter delivery.
Dependencies with Other Projects
None
Risks or Opportunities

Supporting Information

Business Process Impact
None
Acceptance Criteria
Course materials are approved by the pilot team.

FIGURE 6.1   Project Charter

Project Charter as Basis for Scope Change	A project team was developing a website for the organization. During one of the team meetings, the team identified additional features that would really enhance the appearance of the website. The project manager immediately referenced the project charter and realized that the additional features were not part of the original scope. Although these additional features could enhance the final product, just adding them at will would have been bad for the project. Uncontrolled scope changes can cause any project to be late or go over budget. The correct response is to do change control, identify the impact of adding the new features, and obtain approval from the sponsor.

Project Charter Lite Components

An abbreviated charter, referred to in this book as a project charter lite, can be used for simple projects. It consists of the following:

- **Project Objectives**—State what the project will achieve. The project objectives define the business need or opportunity.
- **Stakeholders**—Identify the persons who are actively involved in the project. They include the project sponsor, project manager, and any key stakeholders.
- **Project Scope**—Specify what is included and what is not included in the project.
- **Major Deliverables**—State the major results, goods, or services that will be produced as part of the project.
- **Assumptions**—Identify factors that are considered true, real, or certain.
- **Constraints**—Identify restrictions that limit project options.
- **Risk Factors**—Identify potential problems that could affect the project.
- **Dependencies with Other Projects**—Identify links to other projects.
- **Acceptance Criteria**—Explain how you will know that the project is considered complete and successful.

Project Charter Lite Example

At the beginning of May, Ty was given an assignment to prepare a project management process presentation. This half-day presentation would be given to existing clients free of charge and would serve as a marketing tool for the upcoming project management course.

Ty wanted to be clear about the assignment, so the first thing he did was develop a project charter lite, shown in Figure 6.2.

Project Charter Lite

Project Number	Project Name		
A-TJ06	Project Management Process Presentation		
Prepared by		Date	Project Type
Ty James		5/1/XX	Simple

Project Description

Project Objectives
Develop a project management process presentation to serve as a marketing tool for our project management introduction course.
Stakeholders
Project Scope
In Scope: project management process theory
Out of Scope: project management application
Major Deliverables
Presentation Slides, Activities, Handouts
Assumptions
The pilot team from the project management overview course will review the presentation.
Constraints
Material must be consistent with the project management overview course
Risks or Opportunities
Dependencies with Other Projects
Acceptance Criteria
Presentation approved by the pilot team.

FIGURE 6.2   Project Charter Lite

PROJECT ROLES AND RESPONSIBILITIES

The project manager must identify the project stakeholders at the beginning of the project. In addition to the project manager, the project stakeholders for small projects usually include the project sponsor, customer, and project team. The project manager should define roles and responsibilities for the project stakeholders and obtain their buy-in.

Clarifying expectations at the beginning of the project makes it easier to manage expectations throughout the project. Small projects in particular need to have roles and responsibilities communicated because team members will be working on other projects or operational activities and might not intuitively know their project responsibilities or the short timeframe in which they must occur. Also, with small teams there might not be a backup resource, and lack of communication could result in a project delay.

Small projects usually do not require a steering committee or oversight committee. These committees consist of high-level organizational leaders who represent the decision-making bodies that provide direction for the course of a project. For small projects the project sponsor is normally all that is required to make key project decisions and determine the project direction.

Sponsor

The *sponsor* initiates the project and is responsible for its overall success. The project sponsor provides financial resources, approves project plans, and is responsible for removing organizational barriers that might impede project progress. For small projects the project sponsor may be the project manager's direct supervisor.

Customer

The *customer* is the person who will use the outcomes of the project. For small projects the sponsor and the customer might be the same person. If the sponsor and customer are not the same person, it is important to engage the customer in the initiating process. The customer is responsible for providing input during the planning phase, contributing to problem-solving and decision-making efforts, and taking ownership of the final product.

Project Manager

The *project manager* is responsible for achieving the project objectives. The project manager decides on the project management process components, defines and documents the project, monitors project progress, communicates with all project stakeholders, and manages change. *Project manager* might not be the person's formal title, although this person will assume the project manager's responsibilities as defined in the SSPM project methodology.

Project Team

A *team* is two or more people who share a common goal and work in a cooperative effort to get a common job done. More specifically, the team members work together to complete the project deliverables. Small projects might have five or fewer team members who are considered part-time resources on the project. Team members are sometimes referred to as subject matter experts.

LEADERSHIP CONNECTION

Leadership activities that occur during the initiation phase include:

- Create and nurture the project vision. If project management is typically not used on small projects, the project manager can provide the vision of using project management for small projects and motivate others to use the project management process and tools.
- Map the project objective to the business goal.
- Secure project resources.
- Identify project stakeholders and define the roles and responsibilities of project team members.
- Set up communications. The project manager must determine, how often, by what means, and with which stakeholders to communicate.
- Gather project information through a series of surveys, questionnaires, interviews, review of outcomes from previous projects, and observation of current operations. Information gathering is a key activity because it allows the project manager to determine the project needs, identify project stakeholders, and clarify expectations.

KEYS FOR INITIATING SUCCESS

Keys for initiating success include:

- Engage project stakeholders early in the process and keep them engaged throughout the life of the project.
- Remember that the project charter sets the stage for the planning phase and should include input from all key stakeholders.

INITIATION PROCESS GUIDE

Description

Initiation defines and authorizes the project or a project phase.

Purpose

The purpose of project initiation is to perform the activities necessary to start up the project.

Inputs

- Project Request
- Requirements Overview
- Project Proposal

Tools and Templates

- Project Charter Instructions
- Project Charter Template
- Project Charter Lite Template

Outputs

- Project Charter or Project Charter Lite

Procedures

1. Obtain copies of pre-project documents.
2. Interview project sponsor and other stakeholders.
3. Prepare project charter.
4. Review project charter with stakeholders.
5. Obtain approval from project sponsor to begin planning.

CHAPTER

7

Planning for Small Projects

Defining the work and identifying the resources necessary to complete the project are important. Planning allows you to define what you are going to do, when you are going to do it, and how the project goals will be accomplished. Unfortunately, planning is often viewed as tedious and time-consuming. The response to planning is often that there is no time to plan or that planning is not needed. Either of these responses will set the project manager up for problems later on in the project. Documenting planning activities provides the project manager the opportunity to communicate to project stakeholders, obtain support from team members, and set up a basis on which to analyze and manage the impacts of change.

For a small project, the planning cycle should be short. Scalability is especially important during planning. The effort required to plan the project depends on the type and amount of information and the level of detail that needs to be communicated. The duration required to plan depends on the length of time necessary to discover and document the information, as well as the time required to gain agreement with the sponsor on scope, schedule, and cost.

PLANNING PROCESS SUMMARY

Planning is an iterative process. It should be repeated as new information becomes available. Planning is critical for project success because this is where the project manager defines and documents the project details. These details are then used as the means to manage the project. The planning process allows the project manager to develop all the necessary planning documents, including the work breakdown structure (WBS), project schedule, budget, risk response plan, and communications plan, all of which can then be incorporated into a formal project plan. Some people mistake the project schedule for the project plan, when in reality the project schedule is only one of the necessary planning documents.

Small projects might not require developing a formal project plan or fully developed planning documents. The SSPM process uses a combination of fully developed planning documents and interim planning documents that allows for flexibility in the planning process.

Top-down planning is appropriate for small projects. Top-down planning is starting at the highest level and then adding additional levels as needed. The size of the project determines whether high-level planning at the deliverable level is sufficient or whether more detailed planning is required.

PLANNING PROCESS STEPS

Planning process steps include:

1. Prepare for planning activities.
2. Develop a work breakdown structure (WBS).
3. Develop a deliverable list and task list.
4. Estimate effort and duration.
5. Develop a project schedule.
6. Identify costs.
7. Identify, assess, and respond to risks.
8. Develop communications documents.
9. Develop project plan.
10. Obtain sponsor's approval.

Step 1: Prepare for Planning Activities

The project manager begins the planning process by reviewing the project charter or project charter lite and any documents used as part of the pre-project or development process methodology, such as the project request, project definition, project initiation, or project proposal. If background information or other supporting documents are available, the project manager should review them as well.

This is also a good time for the project manager to review lessons learned from previous projects. Reviewing lessons learned prepares the project manager for problems that might occur on the current project. Early detection of problems or risks allows for more options in developing a risk-mitigation strategy. The project manager should prepare to incorporate lessons learned information into the planning sessions, especially the risk planning session.

The project manager should prepare to engage the project team. The people who will do the work should always be a part of the planning process because they have the information on how and when the work can be completed. Planning sessions are an excellent way to obtain input from the project team. The project manager should identify the participants, prepare a planning session agenda, provide advance copies of the project charter to all participants, and develop a WBS strawman to use to facilitate the planning discussion. (A strawman is a temporary document or item that is used as a starting point and is intended to be replaced when more information becomes available.) Separate planning sessions may be held for developing the WBS, estimating effort and duration, and identifying and assessing risk.

Finally, the project manager should be prepared to share with the team the scope change process and issue escalation process. These two processes should always be reviewed at the beginning of the project and should be thoroughly understood by all project team members.

Step 2: Develop a Work Breakdown Structure (WBS)

Step 2 of the SSPM planning process is to develop a WBS. Developing a WBS is the process of identifying high-level deliverables and then decomposing them into smaller, more manageable components. The WBS can be a simple hierarchy showing only major or high-level deliverables, or it can be more detailed and contain lower-level deliverables. The intent is not to become too detailed but to make sure all the project components are included. In some cases one level of deliverables is all that is needed. Defining the deliverables, even on a small project, helps the project manager to know not only know what should be included but also what should not be included.

The WBS Defined

The WBS is a tool for breaking a project down into its component parts. Building a WBS helps to illustrate project scope, create schedule and cost estimates, assign resources, and provide a basis for control. As stated in the *PMBOK® Guide*, Third Edition, a WBS is a deliverable-oriented grouping of project elements that organizes and defines the total work scope of the project. It is a top-down decomposition of deliverables, where each descending level represents an increasingly detailed definition of the project work.

The WBS for the Project Management Overview course, which was used as an example in Chapters 4 and 6, is shown in Figure 7.1.

Developing a WBS

The following are steps for developing a WBS:

1. Begin by listing the end product. There is only one box at this level.
2. Identify major deliverables. For small projects this might represent the major components of the project.
    2.1. Make sure major deliverables encompass all the work to be conducted on the project.
    2.2. Establish a numbering scheme that shows the hierarchical relationship.
       As identified in Figure 7.1, the major deliverables are 1.0 Instructional Design Planning, 2.0 Course Design, 3.0 Course Development, 4.0 Pilot. and 5.0 Project Management.

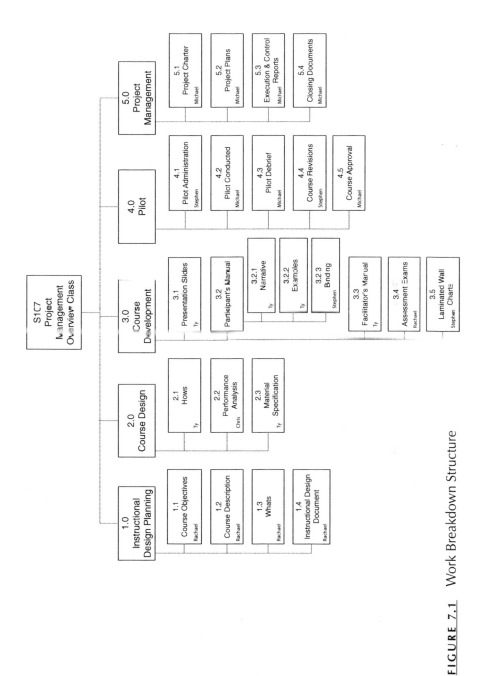

FIGURE 7.1   Work Breakdown Structure

3. Meet with stakeholders to review the major deliverables.
4. Decompose major deliverables to a level of detail sufficient for the project. For small projects, two levels might be all that is needed. Not all deliverables need to be symmetrical in terms of the number of levels developed. Some deliverables will have more levels than others.

   Deliverable 3.0 Course Development is decomposed into five deliverables: 3.1 Presentation Slides, 3.2 Participant's Manual, 3.3 Facilitator's Manual, 3.4 Assessment Exams and 3.5 Laminated Wall Charts. Also note that deliverable 3.2 is further decomposed into three deliverables: 3.2.1 Narrative, 3.2.2 Examples and 3.2.3 Binding.

   Deliverable 3.2 was the only deliverable the needed to be decomposed to a lower level; the other deliverables stopped at two levels.
5. Assign a coding scheme. The numbering scheme should represent the hierarchical structure.
6. Continue to work with the stakeholders to refine the WBS.
7. Assign responsibility for deliverables at the lowest level.

Note: The WBS does not necessarily designate sequence; however, deliverables can be arranged in sequential order if the first level of the WBS represents the project life cycle phases. The first level of the WBS could also represent major project activities.

Another way to develop a WBS is to have the team create it as part of a project planning session. Before the meeting the project manager can create a WBS strawman and distribute it to the team along with the project charter for review. During the meeting the project manager or meeting facilitator should:

1. Review the project charter with the team with a focus on the project scope.
2. Distribute sticky notes to team members.
3. Have the team list one deliverable per sticky note.
   3.1. Place sticky notes on chart paper on the wall.
   3.2. Organize the notes into high-level and lower-level deliverables.

4. Update the WBS by adding or removing deliverables. (Include a heading for out-of-scope deliverables.)

    Recall the example of the Project Management Overview course that has been used previously in this book. In order to develop the WBS for the project of creating the class, the team brainstormed the deliverables. After all of the possible deliverables were identified, the team identified the five major deliverables and then organized the remaining subordinate deliverables. Some deliverables were discarded because they were duplicates or covered by the remaining deliverables. Some deliverables were added because, after organizing the structure, it became apparent what was missing. If out-of-scope deliverables are known at this time, a separate heading titled "Out of Scope" can be included without the relationship lines.

5. Have team members assign responsibility at the lowest level.

Guidelines for Developing a WBS

When developing a WBS, remember the following:

- Deliverables should be expressed as nouns.
- Each WBS element should represent a single tangible deliverable.
- If a deliverable is broken down, it should contain at least two sub or interim deliverables.
- The same deliverable may not be listed twice.
- Ownership should be assigned at the lowest level, and only one person should be assigned to the deliverable.
- The WBS does not contain tasks.
- You should stop breaking down the work when you reach a level low enough to estimate the effort and cost.

Using a WBS

The WBS helps the project manager focus on how to achieve project goals, and it can be used in numerous ways:

- As a communication tool to show how the project deliverables are organized
- To show how much time it will take to complete each deliverable, and therefore how much time it will take to complete the project
- To show how much each deliverable will cost, and therefore how much the project will cost
- As a starting point for team members to define their tasks

WBS Outline

A WBS can be produced without a charting application. Although the graphical representation provided by an organization chart display is preferred because it is easy to read, a WBS can be produced in a text outline format (Figure 7.2). The outline format shows the numbering scheme and the deliverables. Higher-level deliverables are shown as main headings, and lower-level deliverables are indented underneath them. The WBS outline can be contracted or expanded to fit the needs of the project. For example, you might display only the highest-level deliverable, the high- and low-level deliverables, or all levels of deliverables and tasks for specific deliverables.

Making the WBS Planning Session Fun	You can make the WBS planning session fun by: • Color coding the WBS to represent specific areas, phases, or deliverables of the project by using different color sticky notes. • Using color dots to represent resources instead of writing the resource name. • Using color markers to represent areas, phases, or deliverables. • Allowing team members to organize the deliverables into categories. • Providing trinkets for the team to play with during the session.

S107 Project Management Overview Course

WBS	Activity/Task
1	**Instructional Design Planning**
1.1	Course Objectives
1.2	Course Description
1.3	Whats
1.4	Instructional Design Document
2	**Course Design**
2.1	Hows
2.2	Performance Analysis
2.3	Material Specification
3	**Course Development**
3.1	Presentation Slides
3.2	Participant's Manual
3.2.1	Narrative
3.2.2	Examples
3.2.3	Binding
3.3	Facilitator's Manual
3.4	Assessment Exams
3.5	Laminated Wall Charts
4	**Pilot**
4.1	Pilot Administration
4.2	Pilot Conducted
4.3	Pilot Debrief
4.4	Course Revisions
4.6	Course Approval
5	**Project Management**
5.1	Project Charter
5.2	Project Plans
5.3	Execution & Control Reports
5.4	Closing Documents

FIGURE 7.2　WBS Outline Format

Step 3: Develop a Deliverable List and Task List

The deliverable/task list is an outline of the deliverables and the associated tasks. A *task*, the lowest level in the list, indicates the steps or actions required to complete the work. This document can also show who is responsible for completing the deliverable or task.

Depending on the size of the small project, more detailed planning might be necessary. The deliverable/task list can also be expanded to show duration and effort, which will be discussed in the next sections. There might not be time or a need to create a detailed project schedule for small projects, and simple projects certainly don't need a detailed project schedule. The deliverable/task list provides a quick means to define the project activities, allowing for a form of control. The project manager should develop a task list for each deliverable and then estimate the effort, duration, and cost for each deliverable. Again, the level of detail depends on the needs of the project.

Versions of the deliverable/task list are shown as Figures 7.3 and 7.4. Both lists are partial lists from the example Project Management Overview course. Figure 7.3 shows deliverables and tasks. Figure 7.4 is more detailed and includes resources, planned start and finish dates, and space for a short status statement.

Hours can be added to this document, but usually the timeframe is so short for small projects that start and end dates are enough detail. Simple projects, which have an even shorter duration, might not have an associated budget. However, even in the case of a simple project such as a three-week assignment where the costs are absorbed by the department the project manager is still concerned about deliverable due dates.

Step 4: Estimate Effort and Duration

An *estimate* by definition is a quantitative assessment of the likely amount or outcome. Preliminary time estimates provide information on how long the project will take. The time-estimating process includes effort and duration.

Estimating Effort

Effort is the number of units, usually expressed in hours or days, required to complete a task or deliverable. Estimates should be realistic and reasonable. The use of historical information improves the accuracy of estimates. The project manager should involve the project team in estimating activities.

S107 Project Management Overview Course
Deliverable/Task List

WBS	Activity/Task
1	**Instructional Design Planning**
1.1	Course Objectives
1.1.1	Define Course Objectives
1.1.2	Finalize Course Objectives
1.2	Course Description
1.2.1	Develop Course Description
1.2.2	Review and Revise Course Description
1.3	Whats
1.3.1	Draft Whats
1.3.2	Review Whats
1.3.3	Finalize Whats
1.4	Instructional Design Document
1.4.1	Create Insturctional Design Document
1.4.2	Review Instructional Design Document
1.4.3	Revise Instructional Design Document
1.4.4	**Milestone: Instructional Design Document Completed**
2	**Course Design**
2.1	Hows
2.1.1	Define Hows
2.1.2	Review Hows
2.1.3	Finalize Hows
2.2	Performance Analysis
2.2.1	Develop Exercise List
2.2.2	Finalize Exercise List
2.3	Material Specification
2.3.1	Define Examples and Handouts
2.3.2	Draft Examples and Handouts
2.3.3	Review & Revise Examples and Handouts
2.3.4	Approve Examples and Handouts
3	**Course Development**
3.1	Presentation Slides
3.1.1	Create Slides
3.1.2	Revise Slides
3.1.3	Finalize Slides
3.1.4	**Milestone: Slides Completed**
3.2	Participant's Manual
3.2.1	Narrative
3.2.1.1	Develop Narrative

FIGURE 7.3 Deliverable Task List

WBS	Activity/Task	Resource	Start	Finish	Status
1	**Instructional Design Planning**				
1.1	**Course Objectives**				
1.1.1	Define Course Objectives	Rachael Thomas	2/18	2/22	
1.1.2	Finalize Course Objectives	Rachael Thomas	2/25	2/27	
1.2	**Course Description**				
1.2.1	Develop Course Description	Rachael Thomas	2/18	2/22	
1.2.2	Review and Revise Course Description	Rachael Thomas	2/25	2/28	
1.3	**Whats**				
1.3.1	Draft Whats	Rachael Thomas	2/25	3/5	
1.3.2	Review Whats	Rachael Thomas	3/6	3/7	
1.3.3	Finalize Whats	Rachael Thomas	3/10	3/12	
1.4	**Instructional Design Document**				
1.4.1	Create Instructional Design Document	Rachael Thomas	2/25	3/14	
1.4.2	Review Instructional Design Document	Rachael Thomas	3/17	3/19	
1.4.3	Revise Instructional Design Document	Rachael Thomas	3/20	3/21	
1.4.4	**Milestone: Instructional Design Document	Michael Moore	3/21	3/21	
2	**Course Design**				
2.1	**Hows**				
2.1.1	Define Hows	Ty James	3/13	3/19	
2.1.2	Review Hows	Ty James	3/20	3/21	
2.1.3	Finalize Hows	Ty James	3/24	3/24	
2.2	**Performance Analysis**				
2.2.1	Develop Exercise List	Chris Matthews	3/19	3/23	
2.2.2	Finalize Exercise List	Chris Matthews	3/24	3/24	
2.3	**Material Specification**				
2.3.1	Define Examples and Handouts	Ty James	3/25	3/28	
2.3.2	Draft Examples and Handouts	Ty James	3/31	4/11	
2.3.3	Review & Revise Examples and Handouts	Ty James	4/14	4/18	
2.3.4	Approve Examples and Handouts	Michael Moore	4/21	4/23	

FIGURE 7.4   Detailed Deliverable Task List

Of the numerous techniques for estimating effort, some are extremely detailed and provide more accuracy. For the purposes of the SSPM process, however, we use bottom-up estimating as a quick and simple estimating technique.

Bottom-up estimating consists of starting at the lowest level of the project and working upward.

1. Start at the task level and identify how much time it will take to complete each task. Remember to include in your estimate how many times an activity will have to be repeated to get a more accurate estimate of the time required to complete the task. To keep the numbers manageable, use quarter-hour increments—0.25, 0.50, and 0.75. If you are managing your project using deliverables only, start with step 2.
2. Determine the time for completing the lowest-level deliverables by adding together the times required for the tasks that make up the individual deliverables.
3. Determine the time for completing the higher-level deliverables by adding together the time for completing the lower-level deliverables.
4. Determine the total project time by adding together the time for completing the highest-level deliverables.

Even if the project manager does not have to manage the costs associated with the project, the project manager should still have some idea of the effort required to complete the work. A good visual for showing project effort for small projects is the WBS. The project manager can indicate the time required for all levels.

Estimating Duration

Duration is the number of work periods required to complete a task or deliverable. After hour estimates are complete, the project manager can estimate duration.

Duration defines how long—in hours, weeks, months, and other units of time—the work will take. It includes the effort required to complete the work, along with other factors. For example, the reviewer of a document might require an hour to review the document but is given three days to complete the review. The effort is one hour, and the duration is three days.

To effectively estimate duration, you will need to know the skill set of the resource assigned to do the work. Remember that a less-skilled resource will require more time than an experienced resource.

Step 5: Develop a Project Schedule

Scheduling involves converting the work into sequenced tasks. The project *schedule* provides the planned start and end dates for tasks and milestones. A *milestone* is a significant event in the project, usually the completion of a major deliverable. Small projects planned at the deliverable level will show deliverable start and end dates. Milestones would still represent the completion of a series of major deliverables.

Developing a project schedule could become a burdensome task. Small projects can benefit from a simplified version of a project schedule. The schedule can be managed at a high level by including only deliverables or, if needed, key tasks associated with each deliverable. The project manager needs to decide what information will be shown on the project schedule. For example, is it necessary to show hours? For some smaller projects start and end dates are adequate.

Other key scheduling terms are:

- **Activity**—A grouping of tasks. If planning is done at the deliverable level, each deliverable represents an activity.
- **Activity sequence**—The logical order of the activities or tasks.
- **Parallel**—An activity or task that can be done during the same timeframe as one or more other tasks or activities.
- **Predecessor**—An activity or task that must begin or end before another activity or task can begin or end.

- **Successor**—An activity or task that follows a predecessor activity or task. This is also known as a *dependent* activity or task.
- **Milestones**—Markers that show a point in time; they have zero duration.

The project schedule includes the start and finish dates, effort, expected duration, deliverables, and dependencies for project activities. If the start and finish dates are not realistic, the project is not likely to be finished as scheduled. The schedule development process must often be repeated before finalizing the project schedule. The project schedule should be reviewed and updated periodically to be meaningful.

The project schedule could be viewed using the following documents:

- **Gantt chart**—The Gantt chart, originally developed by Henry C. Gantt in 1915, illustrates project information using a bar chart format. The Gantt chart provides a visual outline of the amount of time a project will take. It is also good for high-level reporting because it shows adequate information in a summarized view.
- **Spreadsheet view**—A spreadsheet displays the project schedule using columns and rows.
- **Milestone chart**—A milestone chart shows only the most significant project events.

Depending on the project's needs, the project schedule might reflect differing levels of detail or contain different elements. If task-level planning is required, the project manager should be careful not to plan too many short-duration tasks. Short-duration tasks should be combined using one week of effort as a guideline. Additional guidelines for defining tasks include:

- If a task is longer than two weeks, split it into more tasks.
- If a task contains multiple resources, develop a separate task for each resource.

Most small projects can be easily planned at the deliverable level, and the order in which the deliverables are listed designates the sequencing. Small projects can also be planned at the major activity level with deliverables as the next level. Formal sequencing might not be required, but the sequence could still be represented by the order listed. This approach eliminates the need for a project management application. Small project schedules can be developed using software like Word or Excel.

Step 6: Develop a Project Budget

The project budget is developed by allocating cost estimates to project activities. The budget can be time-phased to show when the costs should be incurred. Resource costs are the costs associated with people doing the work. The budget can be detailed to show resource costs for each activity. Resource costs can be calculated by combining effort with rates. Other project costs might include equipment, training, travel, supplies, or refreshments.

Step 7: Plan, Assess, and Respond to Risks

PMBOK® defines *risk* as an uncertain event or condition that if it occurs, has a positive or negative effect on a project objective. Positive effects of risks are considered opportunities for small projects; these new opportunities are usually handled as a separate project. For purposes of the SSPM process, we will focus on the negative effects that risk events can have on a project. Risk planning consists of four activities: risk management planning, risk identification, risk analysis, and risk response planning.

Risk Management Planning

As stated in *PMBOK®*, "risk management planning is the process of deciding how to approach and plan the risk management activities for a project." The risk management plan for small projects serves as a tool for the project manager to document and communicate risk management activities.

Because the risk management planning process for small projects is simplified with clearly defined tools, the risk management plan has only a few components. It is a narrative document that describes how risk identification, analysis, response planning, monitoring, and control will be structured.

The risk management plan for small projects includes the following

- **Methodology**—Identifies the approach and tools that will be used to perform risk management on the project.
- **Roles and Responsibilities**—Identifies the project manager, project team, and other stakeholders and their corresponding roles and responsibilities during the risk-planning sessions.
- **Timing**—Identifies when the risk identification session will occur and how often the risk management process will be revisited throughout the process.
- **Reporting**—Defines how the results of the risk management process will be documented, analyzed, and communicated to the project team and other project stakeholders.
- **Tracking**—Identifies how risk management activities will be recorded for the benefit of the current needs, future needs, and lessons learned.

A risk management plan might not be required for small projects, but it would serve as a communications tool to inform stakeholders how risks will be handled. Another option is to define the risk management plan as part of the process and update the plan on the basis of the specific needs of the project.

Risk Identification

Risks should be identified. Risk identification involves determining which risks might affect the project and documenting them. Risk identification should occur at the beginning of the project or phase and should be repeated during the project or phase as risk factors change, new action strategies are considered, and new risks are identified. The project team can identify risk events at a brainstorming session.

Participants at the brainstorming session should include the members of the project team. However, other stakeholders, technical experts, and people with similar experience should also be encouraged to participate. Normally it is recommended that someone other than the project manager facilitate the risk identification session; however, for small projects it is acceptable for the project manager to be the facilitator. A list of risk categories can be used to facilitate brainstorming. Some possible categories are organization (e.g., management approach, policy, structure, culture); project management (e.g., schedule, costs, quality, resources, requirements, controlling); implementation (e.g., testing, integration, training); and tools and technology.

Asking "what if" is important. For example, what if the resources are not available when needed or what if the team is unable to complete a deliverable as scheduled? Risks should be documented on the risk register (Figure 7.5), which is developed during the risk identification process and updated during risk analysis. During risk identification, risk descriptions, categories, and potential responses are added to the risk register.

Risk Analysis

Risks should be analyzed. Risk analysis involves quantifying and prioritizing risks. A simplified process for analysis includes assessing the probability, impact, and priority of each risk using low, medium, and high ratings. Risks are normally prioritized in a team session, but depending on the size of the project and the number of risks, the project manager might end up working alone.

- *Risk probability* is the likelihood that a risk will occur. Probability should be classified as low, medium, or high. Risks with zero probability of occurrence should be discarded. Risks with 100 percent probability of occurrence are not really risks because by definition a risk is the chance that an adverse event will occur, and without the element of chance, there is no risk. These items are actually assumptions and should be treated as such.

Risk Register

Project Number	Project Name		Date
S107	Project Management Overview Course		
Prepared by	Customer/End User		Project Type
Michael Moore	Training Department		Small
Project Manager		Project Sponsor	
Michael Moore		Mark Johnson	

Number	Status	Category	Risk Event	Probability	Impact	Priority	Risk Response	Owner
S107-1		Project Mgmt	The project manager is working on several medium sized projects and may not have the time to work on this small project.					Michael Moore
S107-2		Project Mgmt	The senior trainer who also has course development expertise is looking for new opportiunities and it is possible that we may lose a key resource.					Michael Moore

FIGURE 7.5   Risk Register

Probability Rating	Occurrence	Meaning
Zero	Will not occur	There is no chance that this risk will occur
Low	Unlikely to occur but could	The probability that this event will occur is between 1% and 32%.
Medium	May occur	The probability that this event will occur is between 33% and 65%.
High	Likely to occur	The probability that this event will occur is between 66% and 99%.
Certainty (Assumption)	Not a risk	The probability of occurrence is 100%; it is not a risk but an assumption.

- *Impact* is the effect a risk has if it does occur. Impact should be classified as low, medium, or high. Risks with a zero impact should be discarded.

Level of Impact	Meaning
Zero	There would be no impact if this risk should occur. Therefore, it is not truly a risk.
Low—Little impact	The impact on the project would be minor but would be noticed by the customer or sponsor and would create minor customer dissatisfaction. < 5% time increase or < 10% cost increase.
Medium—Some impact on the project schedule	The impact on the project is moderate and would create customer and/or sponsor dissatisfaction with the project. 5%–10% time increase or 10%–20% cost increase.
High—Major impact on the project schedule	The impact is major and could create significant customer or corporate dissatisfaction. It could jeopardize the project. > 10% time increase or > 20% cost increase.

- The *priority* is determined by combining the probability rating with the impact rating.

Probability	Impact	Priority
Low	Low	Low
Low	Medium	Medium

Low	High	Medium
Medium	Low	Medium
Medium	Medium	Medium
Medium	High	High
High	Low	Medium
High	Medium	Medium
High	High	High

This same information can also be displayed in the Probability Impact (PI) risk matrix shown in Figure 7.6.

- *Responsibility.* Each risk must belong to someone on the team. The person assigned the accountability will make sure that the risk is monitored and responses are carried out.

After risk analysis is complete, the risk register should be updated to include the probability, impact, and priority of each risk. Risks can also be grouped by category or sorted by priority.[1]

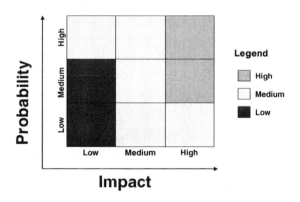

FIGURE 7.6 Probability Impact Risk Matrix

---

[1]Risk assessment tables based on Martin, Paula K and Karen Tate, *A Step by Step Approach to Risk Assessment.* Cincinnati, OH: MartinTate, 2001.

Risk Response Planning

Risk response planning is the process of determining how risks will be handled. Responses should be prepared for all high- and medium-priority risks. Low-priority risks should be documented and monitored. The risk response register should be updated to include more detail for the high and medium risks (Figure 7.7). Risk descriptions are updated with more definition, risk response strategies/plans are identified, and risk owners are assigned.

Step 8: Develop Communications Documents

Communications planning is the process of determining the information and communications needs of the project stakeholders. We communicate to inform, solve problems, and make decisions. Effective communication is vital to project success.

Communications Matrix

The communications matrix (Figure 7.8) describes the communications needs and expectations for the project. It identifies the purpose or description of communication, document or medium used, audience, and frequency.

Responsibility Matrix

The responsibility matrix is a good tool for identifying how and with whom to communicate. It is also a good communications tool because it identifies key stakeholders and their roles in the project. The project manager can see at a glance the type of responsibility each person has for each deliverable.

If the project has a small number of deliverables and a couple of stakeholders, the project manager may choose a more informal method of communicating responsibility.

For small projects the responsibility matrix can show all the project deliverables, or it can be scaled to show just the major deliverables.

Risk Register

Project Number	Project Name		Date	
S107	Project Management Overview Course			

Prepared by		Customer/End User	Project Type	
Michael Moore		Training Department	Small	

Project Manager			Project Sponsor	
Michael Moore			Mary Johnson	

Number	Status	Category	Risk Event	Probability	Impact	Priority	Risk Response	Owner
S107-1		Project Mgmt	The project manager is working on several medium sized projects and may not have the time to work on this small project.	Medium	High	Medium	Have an administrative assistant or project analyst support with some of the routine project management activities.	Michael Moore
S107-2		Project Mgmt	The senior trainer who also has course development expertise is looking for new opportunities and it is possible that we may lose a key resource.	High	High	High	Make sure knowledge transfer is occurring at every phase of the project.	Michael Moore

FIGURE 7.7   Updated Risk Register

and current project schedule, project directory, status reports, risk response plan, and change requests.

Even with the use of a project notebook, an electronic filing system is used. The project manager should define the file structure and location early in the project and store the documents as they are completed.

Barriers to Communication

A conversation consists of at least two parties, each of which has individual wants and needs. If these wants and needs are not the same for both parties, they can present barriers to the message being received. Barriers to effective communication include:

- Not listening, or hearing only what you want to hear
- Sender and receiver having different perceptions
- Words meaning different things to different people
- Ignoring nonverbal cues

Step 9: Develop a Project Plan

The *project plan* is a formal, approved document that defines how the project is executed, monitored, and controlled. It may be a summary or a detailed plan and may contain some or all of the planning documents. Because planning is an iterative process, the project plan is often revised several times through drafts, reviews, and revisions. The final version of the project plan is approved by the project sponsor and baselined to preserve performance measurements.

The baseline plan is the approved plan for the project work against which project execution is measured. Any deviations from this plan appear in the reports used to monitor and control project activities.

The project plan includes:

- WBS
- Responsibility matrix

- Project schedule
- Project budget
- Risk management plan
- Risk response plan
- Communications plan or matrix

Small projects might not require a formal project plan. The subsidiary or standalone version of some or all of the plans is enough to manage the projects. Subsidiary plans are also baselined and used to track project performance. In the absence of a formal project plan, key planning documents are approved by the project sponsor.

Step 10: Obtain Sponsor Approval

After you have completed your planning documents and reviewed them with the project team and other project stakeholders, you must obtain approval from the project sponsor. You are now ready to work on completing the deliverables.

LEADERSHIP CONNECTION

The project manager is responsible for creating an environment where the members can share project information. Planning leadership activities include:

- Select the appropriate level of process, including the right tools, and make sure the team is aware of and follows the processes.
- Engage the right people at the right time.
- Identify and plan for the use of resources.
- Define the project and develop good plans with realistic schedules.
- Hold a project kickoff meeting. Incorporate team-building activities to motivate the team to work together.
- Facilitate planning sessions.
- Obtain sponsor approval.

KEYS FOR PLANNING SUCCESS

Keys for planning success include:

- Plan to plan and be prepared to replan.
- The people who will be doing the work should help to plan the work.
- Use brainstorming sessions to engage the team.
- Use decision-making tools and techniques to facilitate the planning process. Remember that the earlier you identify a problem, the easier it is to solve.
- Include more than the project schedule in the project plan; include all the planning documents.
- Be aware of logical relationships and plan for them. By default most relationships are finish-to-start, where the successor depends on the finish of the predecessor. Other relationships to consider carefully are finish-to-finish (the finish of the successor depends on the finish of the predecessor) and start-to-start (the start of the successor depends on the start of the predecessor). A column can be added to the project schedule to indicate task or deliverable dependencies.
- If project management software is not available, do planning for small projects by using word processing or spreadsheet software applications. A WBS can easily be drawn by hand or developed using an outline format.
- Negotiate for key project resources.
- Use lessons learned from previous projects at the start of new projects.
- Keep project documents in a project notebook, and set up an electronic filing system at the beginning of the project.
- Remember that if you do not plan, you will not have what you will need to keep the project in control.

PLANNING PROCESS GUIDE

Description

Planning is important to ensure that a project can be delivered on time, within budget, and according to specifications. The amount of planning performed should be commensurate with the scope of the project and the usefulness of the information developed. The planning process defines and refines objectives, and plans the course of action required to attain the objectives and scope that the project was undertaken to address.

Purpose

The purpose of the planning process is to define the work and identify the resources necessary to complete the project.

Inputs

- Project Charter

Tools and Templates

- WBS Instructions
- Deliverable/Task List Template
- Project Schedule Guidelines
- Risk Identification and Analysis Guidelines
- Risk Management Plan Template
- Risk Identification Guidelines (including risk categories, information gathering, and brainstorming techniques)
- Risk Register Template
- Risk Analysis Guidelines (including probability and impact scales, and probability and impact table)
- Communication Matrix Template
- Responsibility Matrix Template
- Project Plan Template

Outputs

- WBS (graphical or outline)
- High-Level Deliverable List
- Detailed Deliverable/Task List
- Project Schedule
- Project Budget
- Risk Register
- Communications Plan
- Project Plan

Procedures

1. Prepare for planning activities.
2. Develop a work breakdown structure (WBS).
3. Develop a deliverable list and task list.
4. Estimate effort and duration.
5. Develop a project schedule.
6. Develop a project budget.
7. Identify, analyze, and plan responses to risks.
8. Develop communications documents.
9. Develop a project plan.
10. Obtain sponsor approval.

8

Planning for Simple Projects

Simple projects that involve three or fewer people and occur over a short period do not need a lot of planning. These projects have very few task dependencies and no dependencies with other projects. In most cases, they produce three or fewer deliverables.

But simple projects still benefit from planning. You still need to define how you will achieve the objective, who will do the work, when the work will get done, and, if necessary, what it will cost.

STEP 1: PREPARE FOR PLANNING ACTIVITIES

Using the tools designed for small projects could overcomplicate the planning process for simple projects. Using nothing, however, will cause the project manager to quickly lose focus on the project objective. The process that follows assumes that simple projects have little to no risk and that the costs do not have to be tracked by the project. For example, an assignment to revise a process could be considered a departmental activity, with costs absorbed as part of the base or departmental budget.

The project manager begins the planning process by reviewing the project charter lite and any documents that provide background information on the project. The project manager should also take the time to review lessons learned from previous projects.

An abbreviated planning process for simple projects includes developing a WBS or deliverable list. After the deliverables are defined, depending on the size of the project, the project manager should develop an action plan, a to do list, or both. If more detailed planning is required, the project manager should use the small project planning tools.

STEP 2: DEVELOP A WBS

The WBS is a good tool for showing the components of a simple project, and it should be broken down to the level of detail that will be used to execute the project. Refer to Chapter 7 for more WBS details. Figure 8.1 is an example of a WBS that includes responsibility and hours.

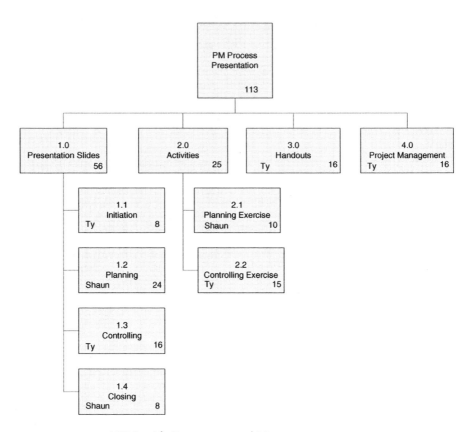

FIGURE 8.1   WBS with Resources and Hours

A more abbreviated activity would be to develop just a deliverable list. The spreadsheet version of the project schedule can also be used to show summary or activity-level project information for deliverables, tasks, resources, effort, and cost, if necessary.

STEP 3: DEVELOP AN ACTION PLAN OR TO DO LIST

An action plan (Figure 8.2) is a list of activities required to complete a deliverable. Action items are usually completed within a couple of weeks, the usual duration of a simple project deliverable. It is a good practice to keep track of the work associated with simple projects because tracking helps to ensure that nothing is missed. A simple project might have three deliverables. The action plan would show the three deliverables and the activities for each deliverable, when the activities will be done, and by whom they will be done. An action plan is similar to a deliverable/task list.

A to do list is a list of all the tasks you need to carry out for a particular period. It combines tasks from different projects. Tasks on the to do list are prioritized so you can do the tasks in order of importance.

LEADERSHIP CONNECTION

- Select the appropriate level of process.
- Engage stakeholders in the planning sessions.

KEYS FOR PLANNING SUCCESS

- Do some form of planning even for the simplest projects.

**Project Management Process Presentation
Action Plan**

WBS	Activity	Resource	Start	Finish	Status
1	Presentation Slides				
1.1	Initiation				
	Develop Initiation Slides	Pat	5/2	5/2	
	Finalize Slides	Pat	5/8	5/12	
1.2	Planning				
	Develop Planning Slides	Shaun	5/2	5/5	
	Finalize Planning Slides	Shaun	5/8	5/12	
1.3	Controlling				
	Develop Controlling Slides	Pat	5/2	5/3	
	Finalize Controlling Slides	Pat	5/9	5/12	
1.4	Closing				
	Develop Closing Slides	Shaun	5/4	5/5	
	Finalize Closing Slides	Shaun	5/9	5/12	
2	Activities				
2.1	Planning Exercise				
	Develop Planning Exercises	Shaun	5/8	5/10	
	Finalize Planning Exercises	Shaun	5/13	5/14	
2.2	Controlling Exercise				
	Develop Controlling Exercises	Pat	5/8	5/10	
	Finalize Controlling Exercises	Pat	5/13	5/14	
3	Handouts				
3.1	Develop Handouts	Pat	5/8	5/10	
	Finalize Handouts	Pat	5/13	5/14	
4	Project Management				
	Plan Project Activities	Pat	5/1	5/2	
	Monitor & Control Project Activities	Pat	5/3	5/14	

FIGURE 8.2   Action Plan

PLANNING PROCESS GUIDE FOR SIMPLE PROJECTS

Description

Simple projects are generally short in duration and do not require detailed planning. Some form of planning should be done, however, to ensure that the requirements are understood and that the project will be delivered on time.

Purpose

The purpose of the planning process is to define the work and identify the resources necessary to complete the project.

Inputs

- Project Charter Lite

Tools and Templates

- WBS Instructions
- Action Plan Template
- To Do List Template

Outputs

- WBS (graphical or outline)
- Action Plan
- To Do List

Procedures

1. Prepare for planning activities.
2. Develop a work breakdown structure (WBS).
3. Develop action plan or to do list.

9

Controlling

The plans are all in place. The focus is now on executing, monitoring, and controlling project activities. For small projects these three processes are combined, and for simplicity we are calling them controlling. Keeping all the project documents current is important. These activities should not be overly time-consuming because the choice of tools and techniques in the planning phase was based on the needs of the project. If the process appears to become burdensome, the project manager should make adjustments as necessary.

CONTROLLING PROCESS SUMMARY

The *PMBOK® Guide*, Third Edition, provides the following definitions.

- *Executing* consists of the processes performed to complete the work defined in the project management plan that accomplishes the project's objectives. It is directing, managing, performing, and accomplishing the project work—providing the deliverables.
- *Monitoring and controlling* are the processes performed to measure and monitor project execution so that corrective action can be taken when necessary to control the execution of the phase or project. More specifically, to monitor is to collect project performance data with respect to a plan, produce performance measures, and report and disseminate performance information. To control is to compare actual performance with planned performance, analyzing variances, assessing trends to effect process improvements, evaluating possible alternatives, and recommending appropriate corrective action as needed.

CONTROLLING PROCESS ACTIVITIES

Controlling activities are not sequential. Some occur routinely and some occur if needed. The following is a list of controlling activities:

- Update project schedule.
- Prepare status reports.
- Manage issues.
- Update risk register.
- Review and approve deliverables.
- Manage scope changes if necessary.

Update Project Schedule

The project schedule should be reviewed and updated weekly. Activities that have been completed during the current week should be updated to show a completed status. The remaining activities should be reviewed to determine the focus for the current week. Any activities that are behind schedule should be reviewed, and decisions should be made immediately on how to get back on track. Any additional work details required for management purposes that do not change the project scope can be added. Sometimes the work might be planned at the deliverable level, and task-level information is needed for better control. Include additional details only if necessary. Remember that the more detailed the project schedule is, the more time will be required to maintain it. The goal is to have the right amount of detail for each project.

Even small projects get into trouble sometimes. The project manager should be aware of signs that the project is heading for trouble. For example, if the number of late activities keeps increasing each week, or the planned versus actual variances get bigger, these warning signs should not be ignored. The project manager should work closely with the team to determine the causes. If it is determined that the original estimates cannot be met and new estimates are required, the project manager should follow the change control process.

Prepare Status Reports

Status reporting for small projects can be simple and should occur weekly. The team should update the project manager during team meetings or by email. The project manager should complete a report and distribute it to the project sponsor and other project stakeholders. The status report should include a project description, the overall project status, major accomplishments, project variances, plans for the next period, and project issues.

Traffic light reports provide an overall summary of a project using green, yellow, and red indicators.

- *Green* indicates that the project is on track.
- *Yellow* provides a warning that there is some indication that the project might not meet completion criteria.
- *Red* indicates that the project is in trouble and has missed a key milestone.

This type of status report is valuable because it causes the reader to focus immediately on the problem areas. This status report should include indicators for schedule and cost, along with an explanation for the indicator color. In addition to the summary indicators, this status report should include the same components identified for the simple status report. An easy way to produce a traffic light report is to use the word (green, yellow, or red) as the indicator in the overall project status section of the status report.

Status Report Example

Today is May 16, and Michael has prepared his weekly status report (Figure 9.1). He is somewhat concerned that he might be losing a key resource, and therefore he has given the resource portion of the status a yellow indicator. He has also indicated on the milestone schedule that the participant's manual might not be completed on time. An issue related to this problem was also logged. The narrative for the participant's manual was supposed to be finalized May 16, but it is not complete. The team plans to complete the task next week.

Status Report

Project Number	Project Name	
S107	Project Management Overview Course	
Project Manager	**Week Ending**	**Project Type**
Michael Moore	5/16/XX	Small

Project Objective
Develop a beginning level project management course that can be offered to the general public beginning third quarter 20XX.

Overall Project Status

Schedule	G	On schedule
Budget	G	On budget
Resources	Y	The senior trainer may be leaving the project.

Milestone Status

WBS	Milestone	Planned End	Actual End	Comments
1.4.4	Instructional Design Document	3/21	3/20	
3.1.4	Presentation Slides	4/23	4/23	
3.2.4	Participant's Manual	5/23		If the senior trainer leaves the project, we may not meet the 5/23 date.
3.3.6	Facilitator's Manual	5/30		
4.2.2	Pilot Conducted	6/3		
4.8	Course Approved	6/23		
5.4.4	Project Turnover	6/30		

Issues

No.	Description	Action
S107-1	The senior trainer was offered another position within this company and may not be available to complete this project.	The project sponsor will meet with both department managers to determine if senior trainer can continue working on this project.

continues

FIGURE 9.1 Status Report

Accomplishments This Period

▲ Decided to use a three-ring binder for the participant's manual.
▲ Completed facilitator's manual review.

Plans for Next Period

▲ Assemble the participant's manual
▲ Revise the facilitator's manual
▲ Finalized narrative

Late Tasks

▲ Finalized narrative is late and will be completed next week.

FIGURE 9.1   Status Report (continued)

Manage Issues

It is very important to identify and resolve issues. An *issue* is a point or matter in question or in dispute. It will impede project progress and cannot be resolved by the project team without outside help.

There should not be many issues on small projects; however, if an issue is identified, the project should document the issue and develop a plan for resolving it. Because of the small number of issues, a formal issues log might not be required for small projects. The project manager should communicate the issue and plan immediately to the project sponsor. The issue can be documented in the issues section of the status report. The information should include an issue description, plans for resolving the issue, current status, person assigned, and estimated completion date. There is no need to prioritize for small projects because time is of the essence. Any issue that arises should be considered a high priority that needs immediate action.

If it is determined that a formal issues log is necessary, the issues log should contain the issue, priority, date the issue was identified, name of the person who identified the issue, name of the person assigned the issue, current status, date resolved, and resolution.

The project manager should have a defined issues escalation process. This process should be communicated to and adhered to by the project team. The escalation process should identify the timeframe the team is given to resolve an issue and how to treat issues that the team is unable to resolve within that timeframe.

Update Risk Register

There is very little risk management activity for small projects. However, if risks were identified, the project manager should review the risk response plan periodically. Updates to the plan include identifying additional risks and changes in risk priorities, updating the status, and closing risks that no longer apply.

Review and Approve Deliverables

Small projects usually do not have a formal quality plan. It is important, however, to build quality into the deliverable review and approval process. The two types of deliverable reviews are in process and completed. During the in-process deliverable review, the project manager should meet with the sponsor and other stakeholders as needed to verify that the work performed on deliverables is meeting their expectations. In-process reviews provide an opportunity to make midcourse corrections. During the completed deliverables review, the project manager ensures that each deliverable meets the stakeholders' needs and that the stakeholders are willing to take ownership.

The project manager should receive formal approval for final deliverables. It can be in the form of an email indicating acceptance. A deliverable review and approval log can be used to track the progress of project deliverables. This log can also be used as a contents document that provides hyperlinks to the deliverables.

Deliverable Review and Approval Report Example

It is May 16, and Michael has received and stored the deliverables. He has chosen to use the deliverable review and approval log (Figure 9.2) as a contents document and has hyperlinked the deliverables for easy access.

Deliverable Review and Approval Log

Project Number	Project Name		
S107	Project Management Overview Course		
Project Manager		Date	Project Type
Michael Moore		5/16/XX	Small

Project Objective
Develop a beginning level project management course that can be offered to the general public beginning third quarter 20XX.

WBS	Milestone	Date Received	Status (in process/completed)	File Name and Location
1.1	Course Objectives	2/27	Reviewed by Ty	
1.2	Course Description	2/28	Reviewed by Ty	
1.3	Whats	3/12	Review by Ty	
1.4	Instructional Design Document	3/20	Approved by Mary	
2.1	Hows	3/22	Reviewed by Michael	
2.2	Performance Analysis	3/23	Approved by Mary	
2.3	Material Specification	4/23	Completed by Ty	
3.1	Presentation Slides	4/11	Approved by Mary	
3.2	Participants' Manual	5/9	Prototype in process	
3.3	Facilitator's Manual	5/9	Draft in process	
3.4	Assessment Exams			
3.5	Laminated Wall Charts			
4.1	Pilot Administration			
4.2	Pilot Conducted			
4.3	Pilot Debrief			
4.4	Course Revisions			
4.5	Course Approval			

FIGURE 9.2   Deliverable Review and Approval Log

Manage Scope Changes if Necessary

Change control is managing the scope of the project. Scope changes do not occur often for small projects, but they could include adding or removing deliverables, changing the effort or duration required to complete the work, or changing the project budget. If a scope change is needed, the project manager should document the requested change and identify the impacts on the project in terms of effort, cost, and duration. The scope change request is communicated to the project sponsor, who has to approve the request before any changes to the plan are made.

If the scope change request is approved, the project manager should update the project schedule to include the new activities and communicate the change to the project stakeholders.

Scope Change Request Example

Michael was pleased with the progress the team was making but concerned that the course would not be competitive because many of the competing project management organizations offer three-day introductory project management courses. Changing the project from a one-day course to a three-day course would require approval. Michael filled out a scope change request (Figure 9.3). The change was rejected.

Small projects should not have many changes. In the case of an exception, the project manager should use a change request log to track the changes. The log should include the scope change request number, scope change description, responsibility, date requested, date resolved, status, and resolution.

Signs a Small Project is Heading for Trouble	Here are some signs that a small project is heading for trouble:
	• Due dates are missed.
	• There is no scope control—work is added without assessing the impact and getting approval.
	• Project plans are not current or nonexistent.
	• Project data is disorganized or missing.
	• Project team is dysfunctional.

Scope Change Request

Project Number	Project Name		Date
S107	Project Management Overview Course		3/19
Project Manager	**Project Description**		
Michael Moore	Develop a beginning level project management course that can be offered to the general public beginning third quarter 20XX		

Change Number	Change Title
37	PM Overview Course Increase

Change Description
Increase the project management overview course to last for three days.

Assessment
To adequately cover all of the topics and include hands-on application would take three days. Also, many competitors offer introductory three-day courses

Impacts
The budget will have to be increased and the timeline extended.

Decision	Comments
☐ Approved ☐ Deferred ■ Rejected	We need to meet the third quarter deadline. The possibility of a three-day introductory course will be evaluated in the future.

Approved by:

FIGURE 9.3   Scope Change Request

ACTION ITEMS

Small projects do not require a separate action item log. Action items are unplanned activities that occur during the project and require little effort (usually a couple of hours) and have a short duration (usually no more than a couple of weeks). Most action items are identified during meetings and are assigned to a team member because work is required to answer a question or complete an activity. Action items can be handled in one of two ways: They can be added to the project schedule, or they can be captured and monitored in the meeting minutes. If you need to track action items, refer to Chapter 8 for an example of an action plan.

LEADERSHIP CONNECTION

The project manager is responsible for executing, monitoring, and controlling the project. Controlling leadership activities include:

- Take responsibility for the project.
- Build and empower teams by understanding the stages of team development and responding to the needs of the team.
- Insist that team members use the project management processes.
- Facilitate problem-solving and decision-making sessions.
- Track issues and drive them to closure.
- Initiate project communications with all stakeholders

KEYS FOR EXECUTING SUCCESS

Keys for executing success include:

- Carefully monitor project progress, respond to variances, and manage change.
- Manage issues and risks, and escalate when necessary.
- Have a positive attitude, especially during difficult times.

CONTROLLING PROCESS GUIDE

Description

The executing and controlling processes occur in parallel. Executing is the process of completing the work as defined in the project management plan or planning documents. Controlling is the process of measuring and monitoring project activities so that corrective action can be taken when necessary.

Purpose

The purpose of the executing and controlling process is to define the activities required to keep the project on schedule. Controlling activities are not sequential. Some activities occur routinely and some occur only if needed.

Inputs

- WBS
- High-Level Deliverable List
- Detailed Deliverable/Task List
- Project Schedule
- Project Budget
- Risk Register
- Communications Plan
- Project Plan

Tools and Templates

- Status Reporting Template
- Issues Log Template
- Deliverables Review and Approval Log Template
- Scope Change Request Template

Outputs

- Updated Project Schedule
- Updated Risk Register
- Status Reports
- Issues Log
- Scope Change Request

Activities

1. Update project schedule.
2. Prepare status reports.
3. Manage issues.
4. Update risk register.
5. Review and approve deliverables.
6. Manage scope changes if necessary.

CHAPTER

10

Closing

Projects, by definition, end. When the project is finished, the project manager should finalize all project activities. But what does this mean for small projects? And how much formality does it really take to close a simple project?

CLOSING PROCESS SUMMARY

The closing process is formalizing acceptance of the project and bringing it to an orderly end. The closing process is important not only for current projects but also for the success of future projects. Small projects are easy to close. The focus is administrative closure, more specifically, to deliver project outputs and shut down the work. The project manager should collect project records, analyze project success or failure, gather lessons learned, produce a project closure report, and archive project information for future use.

CLOSING PROCESS STEPS

Closing process activities include:

- Close out project files.
- Evaluate the project.
- Gather lessons learned.
- Produce a project closure report.
- Archive project information.

The project manager should use the project closure checklist to ensure that critical close-out activities are not missed. Note that these are called activities, not steps, because they are not always performed sequentially.

Project Closure Checklist Example

At the end of the project management course project, the project closure checklist will look like Figure 10.1.

Project Closure Checklist

Project Number	Project Name		
S107	Project Management Overview Course		

Project Manager	Project Type	Project Impl Date	Report Date
Michael Moore	Small	6/23/06	6/30/06

Project Management

No.	Description	Cmpl
1	Project deliverables approved	Yes
2	Issues resolved	Yes
3	Final status report produced	Yes
4	Achieved success criteria	Yes
5	Resources released	Yes
6	Completed project survey	Yes
7	Conducted lessons learned	Yes
8	Produced project closure report	Yes
9	Project data archived	Yes

Rationale for Items Not Completed

No	Rationale

FIGURE 10.1   Project Closure Checklist

Activity 1: Close Out Project Files

At this time all the deliverables are complete and the project manager has possession of all required sign-offs. The deliverable review and approval checklist should be complete. The project manager should do the following:

- Review the project schedule to verify that all the tasks were completed.
- Produce and distribute a final status report to project stakeholders indicating that the project is complete.
- Make sure there are no outstanding issues. Any open issues should be resolved, or a decision should be made on who in the operational area will be responsible for resolving them.
- Determine whether any project risks need to be transferred to the operational area.
- Review the project budget and determine what will happen to any excess project funds.

Activity 2: Evaluate the Project

The purpose of the project evaluation is to compare what was produced to what was planned. The project manager must make sure all project requirements were satisfied and that the criteria for success were met. A project survey (Figure 10.2) can be issued to project stakeholders to obtain this vital information.

The project manager must also identify any post-project responsibilities and make arrangements to address them with the appropriate people. This is also a good time to make sure everything is in place for future project audits or performance evaluations.

Activity 3: Conduct Lessons Learned

Whatever you learn from the process of performing the project is called lessons learned. Lessons learned are the documented information that reflects both the positive and negative experiences of the project. Although we are discussing lessons learned as part of the project closing process, in reality lessons learned can be accumulated at any point during the project.

Project Survey

Project Number	Project Name		
S107	Project Management Overview Course		
Project Manager		**Week Ending**	**Project Type**
Michael Moore		6/19/XX	Small

Project Management

No.	Description	SA	A	N	D	SD
1	The project followed the methodology.					
2	The project used the appropriate tools.					
3	Adequate time was spent planning project activities.					
4	Adequate time was spent controlling project activities.					
5	Changes in the project scope were managed.					
6	Project meetings were organized and productive.					
7	The project met its objectives.					
8	There was clear communication for all stakeholders.					

Project Development

No.	Description	SA	A	N	D	SD
1	The appropriate development methodology was used.					
2	Project requirements were clearly defined.					
3	The design followed the requirements.					
4	Project deliverables were reviewed and approved.					
5	Appropriate tests were conducted.					
6	Acceptance criteria was agreed on and documented.					

Key: SA = Strongly Agree, A = Agree, N = No Opinion, D = Disagree, SD = Strongly Disagree

FIGURE 10.2   Project Survey

The project manager should make sure that a lessons learned session is conducted. During the session the participants identify what was learned as a result of using the project management process and what was learned from doing the project work. The four key questions to answer are:

1. What went well?
2. What went wrong?

3. What can be improved?

4. Are there any recommendations?

Team members should participate in the lessons learned sessions, and the project sponsor and key stakeholders should also be invited. The project manager should not facilitate the session or prepare the lessons learned report. Someone not closely connected with the project, such as another project manager or coworker, is a better choice for a facilitator.

It is not enough to conduct a lessons learned session. Lessons learned should be documented and stored for easy retrieval. And lessons learned should be used. They should be reviewed before starting a new project, they should be shared with the project team, and they should be used for risk mitigation. Future projects cannot benefit from lessons learned if lessons learned are not reported for the current project.

If it is not practical to conduct a formal lessons learned session for the small or simple project, the project manager can still capture the lessons learned information and use it for future projects. Figure 10.3 is a simplified lessons learned report that can be used for small projects. It has been partially completed with information from the example Project Management Overview course project.

Lessons Learned Process	Lessons learned should be conducted at a minimum at the end of every project. A lessons learned process should include the following:

- Identify comments and recommendations that could be valuable for future projects.
- Document and share the findings with project stakeholders.
- Analyze lessons for application of results.
- Store the lessons learned documentation in a repository.
- Retrieve the lessons learned documentation for use on current projects.

Here is how to use lessons learned:

- Review lessons learned prior to starting new projects.
- Analyze lessons learned to identify process improvements or training needs.
- Develop risk mitigation strategies using lessons learned.

Lessons Learned Report

Project Number	Project Name		
S107	Project Management Overview Course		
Project Manager		Project Type	Date
Michael Moore		Small	6/30/XX

Project Management Process

Initiation (project charter, project roles, and responsibilities)	
What Went Well	The project charter clarified the objective and scope of the project.
What Went Wrong	
What Can Be Improved	
Required Action	None

Planning (WBS, project schedule, risk planning, communications, resources)	
What Went Well	
What Went Wrong	
What Can Be Improved	
Required Action	

Controlling (plan maintenance, issues management, risk management, performance reports, change control, stakeholder management, teambuilding)	
What Went Well	Change control prevented scope creep.
What Went Wrong	Not all issues were documented.
What Can Be Improved	A separate issues log should be used to better track the issue status.
Required Action	Create a separate issues log.

Closing (project evaluation, lessons learned, project archives)	
What Went Well	Lessons learned session
What Went Wrong	
What Can Be Improved	A more structured document versioning process
Required Action	

Development Process

Requirements	
What Went Well	Requirements were clear.
What Went Wrong	
What Can Be Improved	

FIGURE 10.3   Partially Completed Lessons Learned Report

Required Action	

Design	
What Went Well	
What Went Wrong	
What Can Be Improved	
Required Action	

Development	
What Went Well	
What Went Wrong	
What Can Be Improved	
Required Action	

Implementation	
What Went Well	
What Went Wrong	
What Can Be Improved	
Required Action	

Post-Implementation	
What Went Well	
What Went Wrong	
What Can Be Improved	
Required Action	

FIGURE 10.3   Partially Completed Lessons Learned Report (continued)

Lessons Learned Activities

Here are activities to perform before, during, and after your lessons learned session:

- Have the participants fill out a project survey. Doing so allows them to identify the items that should be discussed during the session.
- Have the facilitator review key project documents in advance and prepare a list of discussion items.
- Set up flip charts with lessons learned category headings.
- Discuss the lessons learned for each category.
- Send the participants a copy of the lessons learned output for them to review and provide additional input.
- Prepare a summary report and distribute it to stakeholders.

Activity 4: Produce a Project Closure Report

For more formality, the project manager can produce a project closure report. This is an optional activity because small projects do not require this level of detail, but it is nice to have all the key project closing information in one document. The project closure report is used to measure project success and provide information for future projects. It contains the information from the project evaluation and lessons learned.

The project closure report should be started near the end of the project and completed after the final deliverable is turned over to the customer. This document can also be used if the project is terminated for reasons other than completion.

The project closure report should include the following:

- **Reason for Closing the Project**—State why the project is being closed: all objectives have been completed, or the project was cancelled and the reason for doing so.
- **Post-Project Responsibilities**—Identify any activities required by the operational area. This section can also be used to list enhancements that were identified during the project but were not within the project scope.
- **Project Performance**
  - *Performance against Objectives*—Describe how the project met the objectives defined in the project charter.
  - *Performance against Success Criteria*—Describe how the project compared to the success criteria defined in the project charter.
  - *Performance against Schedule*—Describe actual performance against the project schedule.
  - *Performance against Budget*—Describe actual performance against the project budget.
- **Lessons Learned**
  - *What Worked Well*—Identify what worked well for the project.
  - *What Did Not Work Well*—Identify what did not work well for the project.

- *What Can Be Improved*—Identify any process improvements or training opportunities encountered during the project.
- *Recommendations*—List recommendations.

Project Closure Report Example

The project is complete. The team completed the project survey and participated in the lessons learned session. Michael has used the results from the lessons learned report, along with other project metric information, to complete the project closure report, shown in Figure 10.4.

Project Closure Report

Project Number	Project Name		
S107	Project Management Overview Course		
Project Manager	Project Type		Date
Michael Moore	Small		6/30/XX

Reason for Closing the Project
Project deliverables were completed.

Post Project Responsibilities
The training department will make future revisions on project course materials.

Project Performance	
Performance Against Objectives	The beginning level project management course was available to be offered to the public beginning third quarter 20XX.
Performance Against Success Criteria	Course materials were approved by the pilot team.
Performance Against Schedule	The project completed on schedule.
Performance Against Budget	The project finished $1,000 under budget.

Lessons Learned	
What Went Well	The use of the project charter clarified the scope. The change control process prevented scope creep.
What Went Wrong	Not all issues were documented.
What Can Be Improved	Issues management
Recommendations	Develop an issues log.

FIGURE 10.4   Project Closure Report

Project Celebrations	The project manager should reward the project team members for success. Some examples of rewards include: • A team luncheon • An after-work reception • Certificates and awards • Personal thank-you notes • Desk accessories • Gift certificates

Activity 5: Archive Project Information

It is important to have a document management system for storing project documents electronically. The system allows easy retrieval during the project and provides historical data for future projects. The project manager should not wait until the end of the project to begin storing project documents. The document management system should include file locations, naming and standards, versioning, retention/purging criteria, and backup instructions.

LEADERSHIP CONNECTION

Closing leadership activities include:

- Bring the project to closure and communicate closure status to the project stakeholders.
- Arrange for the lessons learned session.
- Recognize the project team for a job well done.

KEYS FOR CLOSING SUCCESS

Keys for closing success include:

- Make sure project objectives are met.
- Make sure all deliverables are complete.
- Archive project documentation.
- Celebrate project success.

CLOSING PROCESS GUIDE

Description

Formalizes acceptance of the product, service, or result and brings the project to an orderly end.

Purpose

The purpose of the closing process is to provide the activities to formally close the project.

Inputs

- Updated Project Schedule
- Status Reports
- Issues Logs

Tools and Templates

- Project Closure Checklist
- Project Survey
- Lessons Learned Report Template
- Project Closure Report Template

Outputs

- Project Closure Checklist
- Lessons Learned Report

Procedures

1. Close out project files.
2. Evaluate the project.
3. Gather lessons learned.
4. Produce a project closure report.
5. Archive project information.

Additional Discipline

11

Managing Multiple Small Projects

Managing multiple projects allows the project manager to more efficiently plan and control project activities. When projects are grouped, schedule impacts across projects become more visible. Consolidated reporting allows the project manager to view the progress of the entire project portfolio.

MULTIPLE PROJECT OVERVIEW

Before we get started with how to manage multiple small projects, reviewing some definitions that relate to the multiple project environment is a good idea.

PMBOK® Definitions

The following definitions are reprinted from the *PMBOK® Guide*, Third Edition, with the kind permission of PMI®.

- **Project**—A temporary endeavor undertaken to create a unique product, service, or result.
- **Program**—A group of related projects managed in a coordinated way to obtain benefits and control not available from managing them individually. A program may include elements of related work outside the scope of the discrete projects in the program. A program could also be viewed as a very large project broken into smaller components.
- **Portfolio**—A collection of projects or programs and other work that are grouped together to facilitate effective management of that work to meet strategic business objectives. The projects or

programs in the portfolio might not necessarily be interdependent or directly related.

- **Project management**—The application of knowledge, skills, tools, and techniques to project activities to meet the project requirements.
- **Program management**—The centralized, coordinated management of a program to achieve the program's strategic objectives and benefits.
- **Portfolio management**—The centralized management of one or more portfolios, which includes identifying, prioritizing, authorizing, managing, and controlling projects, programs, and other related work to achieve specific strategic business objectives.

Although program management can consist of managing a number of interrelated small projects, program management is out of scope for this book because small projects within programs are usually managed using the same methodology as the other projects in the program. The focus of this chapter is on how to manage small project portfolios effectively.

SMALL PROJECT PORTFOLIOS

Two types of portfolios are covered in this chapter:

- **A portfolio of related projects** consists of projects of a similar type, organization, or subject matter; for example, small maintenance and enhancement projects, business process reengineering projects, or pre-project efforts for requesting, estimating, and approving projects. These projects often share resources and are formally managed by a project portfolio manager.
- **A portfolio of unrelated projects** consists of multiple projects assigned to the project manager. These projects may consist of some related projects in addition to ad hoc projects and assignments. The project manager can combine these projects into a portfolio, giving the project manager the tools to more efficiently plan, monitor, and control project activities.

Project portfolio management is concerned with selecting and prioritizing projects, along with assigning the project manager. The focus is on controlling the flow of the work. The portfolio manager must take a strategic view and align project selection and performance with organizational goals and objectives. The portfolio manager's role is not the emphasis of this chapter. We specifically look at the project manager's role and responsibilities. The type of portfolio—related or unrelated projects—does not matter. The point is for the project manager to efficiently plan and control an individual portfolio of multiple projects.

PROBLEMS WITH MANAGING MULTIPLE PROJECTS

As a project manager of small projects, you are aware of the importance of using a methodology and tools to manage a single project. You have achieved a level of success with managing small projects and have been awarded the opportunity to manage more projects simultaneously. At first the single project methodology applied over a few projects appears to work. After a short time, however, you become concerned. Some of your concerns are:

- Common resources are assigned to multiple projects.
- Many of your project team members are part-time resources to the project.
- Team members are juggling priorities—they're working on multiple projects and also responsible for performing operational activities.

You know you need to more efficiently manage time and resources. Because time is of the essence, you also need to more efficiently report project progress and manage issues and risks. You notice that several of your resources are shared among several of your projects and realize that you need to better monitor project interdependencies to ensure that your key resources are available when needed.

What to do? You need to be more efficient. You need more control. And you need a tool to communicate project interdependencies.

The time has come to use the SSPM Multiple Project Management Process.

SSPM MULTIPLE PROJECT MANAGEMENT PROCESS

How is success achieved in a multiple project environment? The SSPM Multiple Project Management Process has three major steps:

1. Develop a single project plan for each individual project.
2. Incorporate individual project plans into a multi-project plan.
3. Execute and control the multi-project plan.

Step 1: Develop a Single Project Plan for Each Individual Project

To be successful in a multiple project environment, you must first have a process for managing single projects and use it consistently. This is the reason the first activity in the SSPM Multiple Project Management process is to develop project plans for individual projects. Part II of this book provided a process and tools for managing small projects.

All projects should have a project charter or project charter lite. The project plan or planning deliverables should be prepared based on the needs of the project. However, the planning deliverables must be prepared with process and tool consistency among projects to allow for easy integration into the multiple project process. After the project plan or planning deliverables are developed for the individual projects, additional planning is required to obtain multiple project process efficiencies.

Step 2: Incorporate Individual Project Plans into Multi-Project Plan

After individual plans are developed, they should be consolidated so that the project manager can see the results of all the projects together.

Multiple Project Summary

The multiple project summary is a spreadsheet view of high-level project information. Summary information is obtained from the project charter and project plan. The multiple-project summary is a good communication tool, but its value comes from the project manager knowing what is in his or her portfolio. The spreadsheet can be sorted or filtered based on reporting requirements. Additional categories can be added for more reporting control.

Information to include on the multiple-project summary is:

- **Project ID**—Include the project number.
- **Project name**—Include the project name.
- **Priority**—Use your organization's code or establish your own system for your portfolio. It is important to know where to focus your efforts. The project priority could change due to its phase or the importance of other projects.
- **Category**—*Category* refers to the kind of work done on the project; for example, information system, process improvement, research, or training. Depending on your work environment, categories could include industry, location, methodology, etc.
- **Type**—Identify whether the project is small or simple.
- **Objectives**—State what the project will achieve. The project objectives define the business need or opportunity.
- **Budget**—Identify the approved funding.
- **Estimated completion date**—Identify the estimated completion date. If you are assigned projects that have not started, a column can be added to track estimated start dates.
- **High level deliverables**—List the major deliverables to be completed as part of the project.
- **Project dependencies**—List projects that your project is dependent on or projects that are dependent on your project.
- **Status**—Note whether the project is active, completed, or on hold.

The following information can also be included on the multiple project summary. Including this information is optional because this information could be lengthy. An option is to produce a multiple-project detail report which has all of this information:

- **Scope**—The scope identifies the boundaries of the project by stating what will be done and what will not be done.
- **Assumptions**—Assumptions are factors that for planning purposes are considered to be true, real, or certain.
- **Constraints**—Constraints are restrictions that affect the performance of the project or factors that affect when an activity can be scheduled.

Multiple Project Risk

Small projects are considered low risk; however, after projects are combined using the multiple project process, the project manager might uncover additional project risks. Risk factors common in the multiple project environment include:

- Project manager trying to manage too many projects
- Too many active small projects sharing the same resources
- Interproject dependencies from high-risk projects
- Too many interproject dependencies
- Key resources being shared among projects
- Poor planning on any project in the project manager's portfolio
- Loss of control on any project in the project manager's portfolio

After the risk assessment is completed for the single project, the project manager should develop a portfolio risk register. The portfolio risk register consolidates the project risks for integrated monitoring and control. Sometimes a single project risk may have a low priority, but when viewed across multiple projects this same risk could have a higher priority.

The multiple project risk register should include the following:

- **Number**—Include the risk number. The risk number is the project number followed by the sequential number. For example, if your project number is S150 and this is your third risk, then the risk number is S150-3. The risk number allows you to map the risk to the project.

- **Project name**—Include the individual project name.
- **Status**—Open or closed.
- **Category**—Identify the risk category. A risk category is a group of potential causes of risk. Examples of risk categories are project management, technical, organizational, schedule, cost, scope, or quality.
- **Risk event**—Identify the event or discrete occurrence that may affect the project for better or worse.
- **Probability**—Identify the probability: low, medium, or high. The probability is the likelihood that a risk will occur.
- **Impact**—Identify the impact: low, medium, or high. The impact is the effect the risk has if it does occur.
- **Priority**—Identify the priority: low, medium, or high. Use the tools in Chapter 7 to determine the priority.
- **Risk response**—Indicate how you plan to handle the risk. You can avoid, transfer, or mitigate a negative risk.
- **Owner**—Identify the person responsible for managing the risk.

The project manager now has a consolidated view of the project risks and can determine if any of the priorities need to be adjusted due to other project risks. If project risk priorities need to be adjusted, the project manager should also update the individual project risk register.

Consolidated Project Schedule

The consolidated project schedule is a high-level Gantt view of the projects. This information can be displayed at the project level, project phase level, major activity level, or any combination. The multiple project schedule is a good communication tool. It also makes it easier to control key project activities.

The multiple project schedule has two important components—inter-project dependencies and duration. Inter-project dependencies or logical relationships among projects, phases, or activities should be identified with the appropriate links. Any time a deliverable from one project (regardless of the level—project, phase, or activity) affects the completion of another project, it should be identified on the multiple project schedule. If a project that is not within your control has a deliverable that affects one of your projects or if one of your projects has a deliverable that affects someone else's project, that dependency should also be identified and shown on the multiple project schedule.

Even if there are no project dependences (all the projects are independent), the multiple project schedule allows the project manager to see the timeframe for project activities that could affect resource allocation. A single resource might be assigned to multiple projects that require the resource's involvement at the same time. Being aware of this condition early on allows the project manager to negotiate for resources before either project's completion is in jeopardy. In addition, the project manager is aware of the project management activities required for specific timeframes and will know whether the project management components of the project are in jeopardy.

Step 3: Execute and Control the Multi-Project Plan

Projects should be monitored, executed, and controlled using the methods defined during the planning process. To gain more efficiency and control, the project manager should use the following multiple project management process tools:

- **Consolidated project schedule**—The consolidated project schedule should be updated to show planned and actual information.
- **Multiple project calendar**—A month-at-a-glance calendar should display project milestones and key project activities. The same calendar should be used to record the information for all projects. This document provides a quick, easy-to-read, consolidated view of key project activities. For additional clarity, the project manager can color code the projects and record project information by project color.

- **Multiple project status report**—Status information for multiple projects should be summarized into one document.

LEADERSHIP CONNECTION

Multiple project leadership activities include:

- Take the initiative to develop an individual portfolio for unrelated projects.
- Stress the benefits achieved from applying the multiple project tools.

KEYS FOR MANAGING MULTIPLE PROJECTS SUCCESS

Keys for managing multiple projects success include:

- Use the process and tools consistently for individual projects.
- Ensure that risk planning occurs twice—first while planning the individual project and then again during multiple project planning.

12

Building Effective Teams

A team is a group of people who share a common goal and are striving to get a common job done. The project team is responsible for accomplishing project goals.

TEAMS FOR A SMALL PROJECT

Small projects typically have small project teams of fewer than 10 members. Small project teams might operate with less formality than large project teams, but general team concepts still apply. Effective project teams, regardless of size, have defined roles and responsibilities.

- **Project manager**—The project manager's primary responsibility is to manage the project activities. Basic management includes planning, organizing, leading, and controlling activities that occur throughout the duration of the project. The project manager does not have to be an expert on the technical portions of the project; however, the project manager should be knowledgeable. Other project team members will be responsible for performing the technical activities.
- **Business analyst**—As the primary interface between the project team and the business area, the business analyst develops the project proposal, defines and documents the business requirements, and provides direction during the project. For small projects the business analyst might also perform some of the subject matter expert activities.
- **Subject matter experts**—Subject matter experts have the specific expertise to complete the project work. They design, develop, test, and implement project deliverables.

TEAM CHARTER

Effective teams have operating guidelines, which can be defined in the team charter. The team charter formally recognizes the existence of a project team and describes the conditions under which the team is organized. It is a mutually agreed-upon contract of behavior for the team that defines the mission, team expectations, operating agreement, and escalation process. Specifically, the team charter clarifies to others what the team is expected to do and the team's purpose.

The project team works together to complete the team charter. Components of the team charter include:

- **Team name**—Develop a name for the team. A name allows the team to have its own identity.
- **Project manager**—Identify the person responsible for delivering the project.
- **Team members**—List all team members assigned to work on the project and the areas of responsibility they represent.
- **Mission**—State what the team is trying to accomplish, the purpose for the team's existence.
- **Values**—Develop a team value statement, which includes specific characteristics of importance to the members; e.g., respect, trust, integrity.
- **Administrative guidelines**—Describe how team communications will occur.
- **Ground rules**—Describe how team members will be expected to interact with each other.
- **Decision guidelines**—Describe how decisions will be made, including time limits on discussions and an escalation process.
- **Meeting guidelines**—Describe when, where, and how the team will conduct meetings, including frequency, time, and facilitation tools.

Two optional items for the team charter that are nice to have include:

- **Slogan**—Create a distinctive catch phrase or motto to describe the project.
- **Logo**—Create a graphical representation for the project.

The slogan and logo can be used on project communications or team paraphernalia. Creating a team slogan and logo is also a good team-building exercise.

Some teams might not require all components of the team charter; they might need to have only specific components defined. This is especially true for simple projects. For example, the team members might question their mission and therefore develop a clear, concise mission statement. This mission statement can then be displayed as a reminder to the team of what it is expected to do.

If a team charter is not used, the project manager should ensure that the team is productive and that project goals are being met. If the team becomes unproductive, the project manager should engage the team in developing a team charter, or at least the key components of the team charter that will allow the team to get back on track.

EFFECTIVE TEAM MEETINGS

Small project teams have impromptu, informal, and formal meetings. Impromptu meetings occur on the spur of the moment or with very short notice and offer a quick forum for discussion. They are ideal for discussing specific issues, solving minor problems, or making urgent announcements. Informal meetings are planned and consist of specific team members required to solve a specific problem. Decisions made during the impromptu and informal meetings should be shared with the project team during the formal project team meetings.

For formal meetings to be effective, they should be well planned and organized. The project manager should plan for meetings to occur at a time that is convenient for team members. If it is determined in advance that a meeting is no longer required, it should be canceled. The project team should have a formal team meeting at least once a week, and these meetings should always start and end on time. Remember that meeting participants usually do not mind if a meeting ends early, but overrunning a meeting is often perceived negatively. Formal meetings should have a meeting agenda, defined meeting roles and responsibilities, and meeting minutes.

Meeting Agenda

The project manager should always prepare for meetings in advance. Each meeting should have a clearly defined purpose. An agenda should be distributed to team members prior to the meeting, along with any documents that will be discussed during the meeting. Doing this allows the team members to come prepared. The meeting agenda should include the meeting date, time, location, and purpose. Discussion items should be listed with the time allocation and discussion leader.

Meeting Roles and Responsibilities

It is important to clearly define meeting expectations, including roles and responsibilities. The project team is more productive if it knows what to expect from the project manager, as well as what the project manager expects from it. Although this information might not be contained in a formal document, the following roles and responsibilities should be communicated to and understood by the project team members:

- **Facilitator**—For small projects, the project manager usually serves as the facilitator. Facilitation activities include setting the tone for the meeting, making sure the meeting follows the agenda, engaging team members to participate in the discussion, identifying action items for follow-up, and using the proper facilitation tools.
- **Scribe**—In many cases, for small projects the project manager also serves as the scribe. The scribe takes notes for the team and produces meeting minutes. To keep the team on track and focused, it might be necessary to capture information on chart

paper. The scribe captures the information and distributes it to the team.

- **Timekeeper**—The timekeeper makes sure the meeting starts and ends on time and that agenda items are given the appropriate allotted time.
- **Meeting participants**—The project team should come prepared to discuss the project activities.

Meeting Minutes

Meeting minutes are the official record of what occurred during the meeting. They should be written clearly and concisely. They should include the time and place of the meeting, the names of attendees, the items discussed, the decisions made, and any new issues identified. Action items should also be included, along with the name of the person assigned to follow up and the deadline. The scribe should distribute meeting minutes to the project team and allow a reasonable time for the team to review them and submit corrections or additions. Meeting minutes should be finalized and stored with other project documents.

THE TUCKMAN MODEL

The Tuckman model, developed by Bruce W. Tuckman, a respected educational psychologist, identifies the distinct stages that small groups go through. The first four stages—Forming, Storming, Norming, and Performing—were developed in 1965, and the fifth stage, Adjourning, was added in 1977 by Tuckman in conjunction with Mary Ann Jensen.

These stages can also be applied to small teams. Each stage must be completed for the team to move on to the next stage. When changes in the team occur, it is common to revert to a previous stage.

Stage 1: Forming

During the Forming stage, the team tries to decide on its purpose and explores the boundaries of team behavior. Individual roles and responsibilities are unclear, and team members are busy trying to identify their tasks and how to approach the project work. Common questions are as follows: What are we supposed to do? Who is responsible for completing this activity? When will this project end? As individuals, the team members are driven by a desire to be accepted by the others as they try to avoid controversy or conflict. During this orientation period, team members are extremely polite to each other while serious issues and feelings are avoided.

At this time the team needs structure and relies on the project manager to provide guidance and direction. The project manager should clearly establish roles and responsibilities, and develop a climate of trust and respect for the team. It is important for the project manager to set project goals and to include the project team in the planning process. The team needs to understand the benefit of working together as a team; therefore, the project manager must share relevant information with the team, keep project communications current, and encourage participation from all team members.

Team-building activities help facilitate the transition from operating as an individual to operating as a team. A quick and easy team-building activity to consider is developing a team charter or having the team agree on operating guidelines or ground rules.

Team Identity How does a team develop its own identity? One way is through its team name. Some teams select team names based on the objectives of the team. Others, especially smaller teams, use portions of the team members' personal names as the bases for forming the team name. After the team name is selected, the development of a team logo or slogan adds a special touch to the team's identity. The team members can then acquire trinkets decorated with the team's identity (name, logo, and slogan) for a nice touch.

Stage 2: Storming

The Storming stage consists of conflict. Team members are forced to address important issues; in doing so, they often challenge each other as they express their individual viewpoints. "What about me" and "I want ..." are phrases often expressed by team members. Minor confrontations that are quickly dealt with or glossed over arise. At this stage the team lacks unity and members often react emotionally; cliques and factions begin to form. Some team members observe that it's good to be getting into the real issues, while others want to remain in the comfort and security of the Forming stage.

The team is looking for structural clarity and rules to prevent the conflict from persisting. The project manager should acknowledge conflict and put controls in place to facilitate decision-making and issue escalation. Bad behavior should not be tolerated. Communication skills are important. The project manager should be assertive, actively listen to the project team, and encourage team members to view alternatives.

Stage 3: Norming

During the Norming phase conflict is reduced. The team becomes more established, operating guidelines are in place, and roles and responsibilities are more clearly defined. The team responds well to the guidance of the project manager. The team members also become more supportive of each other as they begin to understand and appreciate each other's skills and experience. Team cohesiveness is established. Big decisions are made by the team, while smaller decisions are delegated to sub-teams or individuals. Team members have a respect for the project manager and also share in some of the leadership responsibilities.

The project manager should encourage team members to work collaboratively. The project manager should keep the team motivated by being open and supportive and providing positive feedback.

It is difficult for some teams to move beyond the Norming stage because team members have had to work hard to reach this stage and might resist any pressure to change—especially from the out-side—for fear that the team will break up or revert to storming.

Stage 4: Performing

Not all teams reach the Performing stage, which is characterized by a state of interdependence and flexibility. The team works well to-gether and the members trust each other enough to allow indepen-dent activity. Roles and responsibilities change according to need in an almost seamless way. Team identity, loyalty, and morale are all high, which allows the team members to use their energy to focus on completing the project objectives.

During this phase the project manager monitors progress and helps the team to understand how to manage change. The project man-ager recognizes and rewards team accomplishments. The project manager must also watch for changes in participation patterns as the team nears the Adjourning stage.

Stage 5: Adjourning

The Adjourning stage is about project completion and focuses on the well-being of the project team. This stage is also referred to as Deforming and Mourning. During the Adjourning stage, team members complete project tasks and plans are made to dissolve the project team. Team members have a sense of accomplishment for what they have done and are glad to have been part of a successful team. Team members also have a sense of sadness over the upcom-ing dissolution of the project team as they individually prepare to move on.

As project team members' project activities come to an end, the proj-ect manager should show sensitivity to team members' vulnerabili-ties, while assisting with their departure from the project. Remain-ing team members should be encouraged to finish the project. The project manager should recognize the team members for what they have accomplished and celebrate the completion of the project.

Tips for Productive Meetings	Meetings cost time and money, but are a necessary communication vehicle for project teams. Successful project managers must have meeting management skills. Here are some tips for holding productive meetings:

- Choose the meeting time and location carefully.
- Distribute a meeting agenda in advance. Include time allocations for agenda items. The time devoted to each item should be indicative of its priority. Discuss the most important items early in the meeting.
- Distribute documents that will be covered during the meeting in advance. Include in your communication the purpose of the materials and how they will be used at the meeting. Let the participants know if they are expected to provide input or approval.
- Keep the meeting on track. Use a timekeeper.
- Engage all participants.
- Control sidebars.
- Use a parking lot to track items for later discussion.
- Use facilitation tools for decision-making.
- At the close of the meeting review next steps.
- Prepare and distribute meeting minutes.

FACILITATION TOOLS

During a meeting, problem-solving and decision-making opportunities can present themselves without prior notice. The project manager must be prepared to respond immediately in order to keep the meeting moving. Some common facilitation tools include:

Brainstorming—The spontaneous generation of ideas. It allows the team to identify a range of ideas before decisions are made. Tips for brainstorming:

- Let ideas flow freely—hold off on evaluating ideas until later.
- Build on the ideas of others.
- Remind the team that there are no bad ideas and encourage everyone to participate.
- Be creative and think in new ways.
- Do not debate.

- Allow everyone to participate and keep the discussion moving.
- Record ideas as they are generated. When using an easel use alternating marker colors.

Multi-voting—A tool to allow the team to identify priorities from a list of ideas. Steps for multi-voting:

- List the items. This list could include the items from the brainstorming session.
- Remind the team of the purpose of the vote—what you are trying to accomplish.

Each member of the team is given a finite number of votes to give to items on the list. Add the number of items and determine the number of votes per person. For lists with more than 10 items, divide the total by five and round up to the nearest whole number. This number represents the number of votes each team member will have. For lists with less than 10 items, give slightly less votes than half the items on the list.

- Team members vote for their top choices.
- After team members have voted, tally the votes in order to arrive at the priorities.
- To add a little fun to the process, team members can be given color sticker dots to use for voting. Team members can place the dot by the item on the flip chart to indicate their choice.

Decision Grid—A matrix of information used to assess a set of ideas in order to make a decision. A rating system is used to score the options. Steps for using the decision grid:

- Identify the criteria for judging potential solutions.
- Identify options
- Rate each option against the criteria. Remember not to rate options against each other.
- Add the scores to determine the solution.

Gap Analysis—A means to identify obstacles to achieving a desired goal. Gap analysis allows you to look at the current state and to identify things that need to be done to arrive at the desired or future state. The steps to perform a gap analysis are:

- Identify the future state.
- Identify the current state.
- Identify the gaps or what's missing.
- Obtain consensus on the gaps.
- Develop recommendations and action plans.

Project Manager as Coach

One of the responsibilities of the project manager is to coach the project team to realize its full potential so that the team can perform the project work. As a coach, the project manager should:

- Help the project team to align with the project goal.
- Set an example for team members. For example, if the project manager wants the team members to attend meetings on time, then the project manager should set an example by being on time.
- Praise and recognize team members for accomplishing tasks.
- Reserve constructive criticism for private conversations
- Give team members the opportunity to share knowledge with other team members.
- Allow teams to come up with their own solutions. Follow through with team ideas to make sure they are implemented.
- Spend additional time with a team when necessary.
- Remain positive, be flexible, and provide support when needed.
- As the team members gain confidence in their performance, they will take on more responsibility for accomplishing team goals.

LEADERSHIP CONNECTION

Team leadership activities for the project manager include:

- Direct the team during the Forming stage.
- Support the team during the Storming stage.
- Coach the team during the Norming stage.
- Delegate project activities to team members during the Performing stage.
- Direct during the Adjourning stage.

KEYS FOR TEAM SUCCESS

Keys for team success include:

- Ensure that meeting minutes are clear and concise, and contain sentences that are short and to the point.
- Provide team-building activities during the Forming stage to help the team make the transition from operating as individuals to operating as a team.
- Use decision-making and issues-escalation processes during the Storming stage to assist with conflict resolution.
- Coach during the Norming stage by using interactive questioning, collaborative goal setting, constructive feedback, and positive guidance.
- Allow interdependence and flexibility among team members during the Performing stage.
- Show sensitivity and appreciation during the Adjourning stage.

CHAPTER

13

The Power of One

As indicated in Chapter 12, a team is a group of people who share a common goal and are striving to get a common job done. Another way to define a team is two or more persons in cooperative effort. The benefits of working on a team include shared ownership and responsibility for project activities, faster response to change, synergy, and personal growth. The purpose of the team is to work together to accomplish the project objectives—so what happens when the project manager has to work alone? What happens when you have to rely on the power of one?

WHAT IS THE POWER OF ONE?

With the power of one, the support, synergy, and sharing realized from working on a team are lost. However, personal growth is still possible. The power of one means one person is solely responsible for the outcome of the project with the power to choose how it will be managed.

The power of one means you have the ability to:

- Use project management to clearly define the project, develop realistic schedules, and manage change.
- Choose the processes, systems, level of detail, and amount of discipline for managing your project.
- Operate in an organized and efficient manner.
- Define quality up front and edit your own work harshly and objectively and from as many perspectives as you can.
- Keep things simple.

Power of One Challenges	A unique challenge for the power of one is for the project manager to use project management processes and tools when no one else is watching. On a small team, you have at least one person who is aware of your project management practices. Operating alone requires additional discipline because it is easy to tell yourself that you know what is going on and you have everything under control. However, if you do not plan you are guessing about how much work you have and how much time you have to complete it. If you guess wrong—and this often happens—you are faced with the embarrassment of having to explain why you missed the deadline or need more time.

ROLES AND RESPONSIBILITIES

The project deliverables must be completed, and initiating, planning, monitoring, executing and controlling, and closing activities must be performed if you want project success. Remember the triple constraints (*on time, within budget* and *according to requirements*). They still apply. In order to be successful now, you must wear multiple hats—you are the project manager, leader, and subject matter expert.

Project Manager

As the project manager, you are responsible for the overall success of the project. It is up to you to determine how and when to apply project management processes, tools, and techniques. As a project management practitioner who understands the value of using project management, you will not omit your project management tasks just because you believe no one is watching.

As the project manager you are responsible for coordinating project activities, which include:

- Deciding on the processes and ensuring that they are followed
- Defining and documenting the project and obtaining agreement

- Monitoring project progress
- Communicating with the sponsor and customer
- Managing change

It is important to manage the processes, which include the project management process and any other development or business processes required to complete the project. Refer back to Part II, Project Management Process for Small Projects, for a simplified project management process for small projects.

Leader

When you operate with the power of one, many of the common problems normally associated with teams are eliminated. For example, personality conflicts, non-team players, bullies, and the like are not an issue. The ongoing team-building process is also eliminated. Leadership, however, is still required. Leadership is discussed in detail in Chapter 3.

As a leader it is important to:

- **Be a visionary**—Create and nurture a vision.
- **Have integrity**—Have words and actions in alignment.
- **Be a change agent**—Be willing to change personally and then create a climate for others to change.
- **Be a problem-solver/decision-maker**—Be able to recognize a problem in its early stages, and analyze and respond appropriately.
- **Have a positive attitude**—Choose to respond to daily situations/challenges with optimism.
- **Have a business orientation**—Understand the culture and where the project fits in achieving organizational goals.
- **Have a high tolerance for ambiguity**—Understand that uncertainty exists and work to provide clarity.
- **Communicate effectively**—Clearly articulate information, and actively listen to others.

Subject Matter Expert

You also have the role of subject matter expert, which requires you to take on the responsibilities of the analyst, specialist, designer, or developer, to name a few. As subject matter expert, you are responsible for performing analyses, gathering business requirements, developing specifications, creating deliverables, and testing and implementing deliverables. To state it another way, you perform all the tasks required to complete the project.

REALIZING THE POWER OF ONE

If you have the opportunity to operate with the power of one, welcome it as a learning experience. Tailor the project management process and tools discussed in Part II of this book to fit your small or simple project. The more you use these tools, the more proficient you will become with your project management practices and the sooner you will be ready for larger projects. As a leader, you want to always show respect for project management. You never know who is watching or what they will see. You want people to know you believe in the process and tools and that you use them because it is the right thing to do. You want to be known for being able to get the job done. The role of subject matter expert allows you to keep your technical and organizational skills current.

Remember that all small projects are a training ground for larger projects. Use every opportunity to develop your skills.

Assignments as Projects	Assignments are really small or simple projects. Treating assignments as projects allows for better planning and more control of resources.

PALM and the Power of One	Project management can easily be applied to a one-person project by using the PALM principle discussed in Chapter 5. For example, a project manger was assigned to develop a presentation in three weeks. The project manager *planned* the project using an activity list. During the three weeks the project manager continually *analyzed* the situation and kept the activity list current. *Leadership* is always important and the project manager took the lead and sent weekly updates to the project sponsor. The project manager *monitored* the project activities and completed the presentation on schedule.

TIME MANAGEMENT

Project management is an exciting profession that places many demands on the project manager. Managing stakeholder expectations, keeping up with technology, managing multiple projects, and wearing multiple hats leaves the project manager with little time, if any, to spare. Effective time management skills are a valuable asset for any project manager looking to achieve project success. The ability to effectively manage time becomes even more critical when you operate as the power of one.

Time management requires discipline. It requires you to write down what you want to accomplish, create lists, and set priorities. The concept of time management is not new, and lots of material exists on the topic.

Following are some common time management techniques:

- **Create monthly, weekly, and daily priority lists (to do lists).** Writing down what you have to do allows you to start thinking about how you will accomplish the activities.
- **Use a document management system.** This will allow you to easily access your files.
- **Organize your workspace.** Your workspace design should be based on your productivity needs. Keep things you use often close at hand. Keep things organized so that you will be able to find what you need when you need it. A cluttered desk makes you look disorganized.

- **Plan every day in advance.** Set aside uninterrupted time for planning every day. Pick a time that works for you, either early in the morning, before you start working, or the evening, when you can plan out your next workday. Planning your daily activities allows you to set priorities for the day.
- **Keep track of due dates.** This prevents you from having to rush to complete your activities at the last minute.
- **Do the most difficult task first.** This forces you to overcome procrastination and helps you concentrate, because you are not constantly worrying about the difficult task.
- **Develop systems that work for you.** Do not let technology dictate. Whether it's time management, document management, or life management, use the tools that provide you comfort and sustained success.
- **Work according to your temperament.** Know yourself. Schedule key activities to fit your productivity pattern.
- **Allow a little time for the unexpected.** Put some slack time in your schedule. If your schedule is too tight, an interruption can throw your entire day off course.
- **Eliminate wasteful activities.** Saying no to wasteful activities provides you more of an opportunity to say yes to productive activities. Try to keep interruptions to a minimum.
- **Choose to be positive.** A positive attitude increases your energy and effectiveness. Find things that motivate, inspire, rejuvenate, and energize you.

Time Robbers Time robbers are events you didn't plan for that prevent you from accomplishing what you really need to get done. Some common time robbers include:

- Interruptions
- Disorganization
- Poor communication
- Waiting for people
- Poor planning

KEYS FOR THE POWER OF ONE SUCCESS

Keys for the power of one success include:

- Use project management because it is the right thing to do.
- Use all small projects as a training ground for larger projects.
- Effectively manage time and find ways to stay motivated.

CHAPTER

14

Transitioning to Larger Projects

Congratulations on the successful management of your small projects. The knowledge and skills you are acquiring from using the Small and Simple Project Management process and tools allow you to become competent in the management of small projects. This chapter presents some of the challenges and issues you will face if you make the transition to managing larger projects.

PROJECT MANAGEMENT SKILLS

The project management skills you are acquiring from managing small projects serve as the foundation on which you can continue to build additional skills. Here are some additional project management complications that you will manage when you lead large projects:

- **Project Management Process**—The processes used to manage projects will increase to include more activities from the nine knowledge areas: project integration management, project scope management, project time management, project cost management, project quality management, project human resources management, project communication management, project risk management, and project procurement management.
  - *Initiating*—Project charters will be more detailed and will require input from more project stakeholders. You may also have to develop a preliminary scope statement which provides a high-level definition of the project. Project and product requirements will need to be documented.

- *Planning*—More planning will be required. You will spend time planning to plan as you prepare for planning sessions to obtain the information for more detailed and formal project plans. You will incorporate budgeting, resource planning, and contracting activities into your project plans. You will use more techniques for risk analysis.
- *Executing*—More emphasis will be placed on quality assurance to ensure that the project employs all of the processes needed to meet the requirements.
- *Monitoring and Control* activities will increase significantly. You will need to keep detailed project schedules current and manage costs and risks. You will produce more types of performance reports—status, variance, metric, trend, and earned value—and manage the needs of more levels of stakeholders. Document control will become very important because you are sharing more critical team documents with more team members.
- *Closing*—Larger projects are more likely to be audited; therefore, project closure is more formal because key project documents need to be retained. At the close of the project you will also be expected to close contracts and release resources.
- Project Management Software—You will need to use a project management application for detailed project planning and control.
- Process Integration—Projects are more complex and will require the incorporation of other processes:
  - *Product Development Process*—You will us a specific industry development life cycle.
  - *Business Processes*—You will become more involved with the use of processes from the impacted business areas.
  - *Change Management*—You will incorporate the behavior activities required to prepare the organization for a change from the current state to the future state.

LEADERSHIP SKILLS

Your leadership activities will increase:

- You will be expected to drive the project to completion. You have to take charge and make sure the work is getting done. When issues arise, you must make sure they are addressed immediately and resolved as quickly as possible.
- You will be leading larger teams, which will require more meeting management and facilitation skills.
- You will be expected to make key project decisions in a timely manner.
- You will be expected to deliver presentations to project stakeholders.
- Your team will be looking to you for answers. Your credibility will be key. Your team members will need to know they can trust you to get them through the difficult times.

PEOPLE, PROCESS, AND TECHNOLOGY

You will have to find a way to balance people, process, and technology in order to truly be successful. This will be a continuous challenge because projects are unique and people, process, and technology are constantly changing. Remember to choose the processes that fit your project, make allowances for technological changes, and get to know the people on your team and allow them to become fully engaged in the project activities.

PROJECT MANAGEMENT KEYS FOR SUCCESS

Description

The following are keys for success when managing small projects.

Process Overview

- Make sure the right amount of process is used for each project. If too much or too little is used initially, be flexible enough to make the necessary adjustments.
- Keep process guides handy for quick reference.
- Integrate the project management process with the product development process to gain more efficiency.
- Lead the way for other project managers to begin using project management on small projects.

Project Initiation

- Engage project stakeholders early in the process, and keep them engaged throughout the life of the project.
- Remember that the project charter sets the stage for the planning phase and should include input from all key stakeholders.

Project Planning

- Plan to plan and be prepared to replan.
- Make sure the people who will do the work help to plan the work.
- Use brainstorming sessions to engage the team.
- Use decision-making tools and techniques to facilitate the planning process. Remember that the earlier you identify a problem, the easier it is to solve.
- Remember that the project plan includes more than just the project schedule; it includes all the planning documents.
- Be aware of logical relationships and plan for them.

- If project management software is not available, do planning for small projects by using word processing or spreadsheet software applications. A WBS can easily be drawn by hand or developed using an outline format.
- Negotiate for key project resources.
- Use lessons learned from previous projects at the start of new projects.
- Keep project documents in a project notebook, and set up an electronic filing system at the beginning of the project.
- Remember that if you do not plan, you will not have what you need to keep the project in control.

Project Planning for Simple Projects

- Do some form of planning even for the simplest project.

Project Controlling

- Carefully monitor project progress, respond to variances, and manage change.
- Manage issues and risks, and escalate when necessary.
- Have a positive attitude, especially during difficult times.

Project Closing

- Make sure project objectives are met.
- Make sure all deliverables are complete.
- Archive project documentation.
- Celebrate project success.

Managing Multiple Projects

- To successfully manage multiple projects, use the process and tools consistently for individual projects.
- Make sure risk planning occurs twice—first while planning the individual project and then again during multiple project planning.

Building Effective Teams

- Make sure meeting minutes are clear and concise, and contain sentences that are short and to the point.
- Provide team-building activities during the Forming stage to help the team make the transition from operating as individuals to operating as a team.
- Use decision-making and issues escalation processes during the Storming stage to assist with conflict resolution.
- Coach during the Norming stage by using interactive questioning, collaborative goal setting, constructive feedback, and positive guidance.
- Allow interdependence and flexibility among team members during the Performing stage.
- Show sensitivity and appreciation during the Adjourning stage.

CHAPTER 13

The Power of One

- Use project management because it is the right thing to do.
- Use all small projects as a training ground for larger projects.
- Effectively manage time and find ways to stay motivated.

Glossary of
Project Management Terms

This glossary contains common project management terms. This is not an all-inclusive list; rather, it includes terms specifically addressed in this book.

The entries with asterisks reproduce, in whole or in part, definitions from the *PMBOK® Guide*, Third Edition, with the kind permission of PMI®.

Action Plan. A list of activities required to complete project deliverables. An action plan also includes when the activities will be done and by whom.

Activity.* A component of work performed during the course of a project.

Adjourning Stage. The fifth stage of the Tuckman Model. The Adjourning stage is about project completion and is also referred to as Deforming and Mourning.

Assumption.* Assumptions are factors that, for planning purposes, are considered to be true, real, or certain without proof or demonstration. Assumptions affect all aspects of project planning, and are part of the progressive elaboration of the project.

Brainstorming. A facilitation tool that allows for the spontaneous generation of ideas. It allows the team to identify a range of ideas before decisions are made.

Character. The qualities built into a person's life that determine his or her response, regardless of circumstances. Character is the inward motivation to do what is right in every situation.

Closing Process. The project activities to bring the project to an end.

Communication Matrix. A document that defines the communication needs and expectations for the project.

Controlling Process. The project management activities required to carry out the project activities, measure and monitor progress, and take corrective action when necessary.

Constraint.* The state, quality, or sense of being restricted to a given course of action or inaction. An applicable restriction or limitation, either internal or external to the project, that will affect the performance of the project or a process.

Customer.* The person or organization that will use the project's product or service or result.

Decision Grid. A facilitation tool that provides a matrix of information used to assess a set of ideas in order to make a decision. A rating system is used to score the options.

Deliverable.* Any unique and verifiable product, result, or capability to perform a service that must be produced to complete a process, phase, or project. Often used more narrowly in reference to an external deliverable, which is a deliverable that is subject to approval by the project sponsor or customer.

Deliverable/Task List. An outline of the deliverables and the associated tasks.

Duration.* The total number of work periods (not including holidays or other nonworking periods) required to complete a schedule activity or work breakdown structure component. Usually expressed as workdays or workweeks.

Effort.* The number of labor units required to complete a schedule activity or work breakdown structure component. Usually expressed as staff hours, staff days, or staff weeks.

Facilitation Tools. Problem-solving and decision-making tools that help team members work together more effectively.

Forming Stage. The first stage of the Tuckman Model. During the Forming stage the team tries to decide on its purpose and explores the boundaries of team behavior.

Gap Analysis. A facilitation tool that provides a means to identify obstacles to achieving a desired goal. Gap analysis allows you to look at the current state and to identify things that need to be done to arrive at the desired or future state.

Initiating Process. The activities to start up the project. Defines and authorizes the project.

Lessons Learned.* The learning gained from the process of performing the project. Lessons learned may be identified at any point.

Milestone.* A significant point or event in the project.

Multi-voting. A facilitation tool that allows the team to identify priorities from a list of ideas.

Norming Stage. The third stage of the Tuckman Model. During the Norming stage team members operate as a cohesive and supportive team.

PALM Principle. A component of the SSPM process that is used for projects that do not need much formality. The elements of the PALM principle are *plan* project activities, *analyze* the situation and ask questions, *lead* the project activities, and *monitor* and control time and resources.

Performing Stage. The fourth stage of the Tuckman Model. During the Performing stage the team works well together with interdependence and flexibility. Not all teams reach this stage.

Planning Process. The project management activities required to define the project activities and determine how the project objectives will be achieved.

Portfolio.* A collection of projects or programs and other work that are grouped together to facilitate effective management of that work to meet strategic business objectives. The projects or programs in the portfolio might not necessarily be interdependent or directly related.

Portfolio of Related Projects. A portfolio that consists of projects of a similar type, organization, or subject matter. These projects often share resources and are formally managed by a project portfolio manager.

Portfolio of Unrelated Projects. A portfolio that consists of multiple projects assigned to the project manager. These projects may consist of some related projects in addition to ad hoc projects and assignments. The project manager can combine these projects into a portfolio, giving the project manager the tools to more efficiently plan, monitor, and control project activities.

Portfolio Management.* The centralized management of one or more portfolios, which includes identifying, prioritizing, authorizing, managing, and controlling projects, programs, and other related work to achieve specific strategic business objectives.

Pre-Project Documents. These are documents that support the pre-project activities and are used to identify the business need and outline the potential project.

Process.* A set of interrelated actions and activities performed to achieve a specified set of products, results, or services.

Program.* A group of related projects managed in a coordinated way to obtain benefits and control not available from managing them individually. A program may include elements of related work outside the scope of the discrete projects in the program. A program could also be viewed as a very large project broken into smaller components.

Program Management.* The centralized, coordinated management of a program to achieve the program's strategic objectives and benefits.

Progressive Elaboration.* Continuously improving and detailing a plan as more detailed and specific information and more accurate estimates become available as the project progresses, thereby producing more accurate and complete plans that result from the successive iterations of the planning process.

Project.* A temporary endeavor undertaken to create a unique product, service, or result.

Project Charter.* A document issued by the project initiator or sponsor that formally authorizes the existence of a project, and provides the project manager with the authority to apply organizational resources to project activities.

Project Charter Lite. A simpler version of the project charter that can be used to formally authorize the existence of a simple project and provides the project manager with the authority to apply organizational resources to project activities.

Project Communication Management.* The project knowledge area that includes the processes required to ensure timely and appropriate generation, collection, dissemination, storage, and ultimate disposition of project information. Project Communication Management activities include communications planning, information distribution, performance reporting, and stakeholder management.

Project Cost Management.* The project knowledge area that includes the processes involved in planning, estimating, budgeting, and controlling costs so that the project is completed within the approved budget. Project Cost Management activities include cost estimating, cost budgeting, and cost control.

Project Human Resources Management.* The project knowledge area that includes the processes that organize and manage the project team. Project Human Resources Management includes activities for human resource planning, acquiring the project team, developing the project team, and managing the project team.

Project Integration Management.* The project knowledge area that includes the processes and activities needed to identify, define, combine, unify, and coordinate the various processes and project management activities within the Project Management Process Groups. Project Integration Management activities include developing the project charter, developing the preliminary project scope statement, developing the project management plan, directing and managing project execution, and monitoring and controlling project work.

Project Life Cycle.* A collection of generally sequential project phases whose name and number are determined by the control needs of the organization or organizations involved in the project. A life cycle can be documented with a methodology.

Project Management.* The application of knowledge, skills, tools, and techniques to project activities to meet the project requirements.

Project Management Knowledge Area. An identified area of project management defined by its knowledge requirements and described in terms of its component processes, practices, inputs, outputs, tools, and techniques.

Project Management Process Group.* A logical grouping of project management processes described in the *PMBOK® Guide*. The project management process groups include initiating processes, planning processes, executing processes, monitoring and controlling processes, and closing processes. Collectively, these five groups are required for any project, have clear internal dependencies, and must be performed in the same sequence on each project, independent of the application area or the specifics of the applied project life cycle. Project management process groups are not project phases.

Project Manager.* The person assigned by the performing organization to achieve the project objectives.

Project Schedule.* The planned dates for performing schedule activities and the planned dates for meeting schedule milestones.

Project Notebook. A document that provides a practical way to organize and easily access project information to allow the project manager to have key project data available.

Project Plan. A formal, approved document that defines how the project is executed, monitored, and controlled. It may be summary or detailed and may be composed of one or more subsidiary management plans and other planning documents. Also known as *project management plan*.

Project Procurement Management.* The project knowledge area that includes the processes to purchase or acquire products, services, or results needed from outside the project team to perform the work. Project Procurement Management includes activities to plan purchases and acquisitions, plan contracting, request seller responses, select a seller, adminster a contract, and close a contract.

Project Risk Management.* The project knowledge area that includes the processes concerned with conducting risk management on a project. Project Risk Management activities include risk management planning, risk identification, qualitative risk analysis, quantitative risk analysis, risk response planning, and risk monitoring and control.

Project Scope Management.* The project knowledge area that includes the processes required to ensure that the project includes all the work required, and only the work required, to complete the project successfully. Project Scope Management is primarily concerned with defining and controlling what is and is not included in the project. Project Scope Management activities include scope planning, scope definition, WBS creation, scope verification, and scope control.

Project Team. The persons who share responsibility for performing project work and accomplishing project objectives.

Project Time Management.* The project knowledge area that includes the processes required to accomplish timely completion of the project. Project Time Management activities include activity definition, activity sequencing, activity resource estimating, activity duration estimating, schedule development, and schedule control.

Project Quality Management.* The project knowledge area that includes the processes and activities of the performing organization that determine quality policies, objectives, and responsibilities so that the project will satisfy the needs for which it was undertaken. Project Quality Management activities include quality planning and performing quality assurance and quality control.

Responsibility Matrix. A document that identifies key stakeholders and their roles in the project.

Risk.* An uncertain event or condition that, if it occurs, has a positive or negative effect on a project's objectives.

Risk Analysis. Quantifying and prioritizing risks.

Risk Identification.* The process of determining which risks might affect the project and documenting their characteristics.

Scalability. The ability to alter the level of complexity of the project management process, the time spent in using the process, and the focus of the process to fit the needs of the project.

Simple Project. A project that is small, straightforward, short in duration, and is completed by a team of three or fewer team members. Simple projects are often called assignments.

Small and Simple Project Management (SSPM). A methodology that includes processes and tools specifically designed for managing small and simple projects.

Small and Simple Project Management Process. A logical grouping of project management processes designed specifically for use on small and simple projects. The four project management phases are initiate, plan, control, and close.

Small and Simple Project Management Multiple Project Management Process. A logical grouping of project management processes designed specifically for use on multiple small projects.

Small Project. A small project is generally one that is short in duration, typically lasting less than six months; is part-time in effort hours; has 10 or fewer team members; involves a small number of skill areas; has a single objective and a solution that is readily achievable; has a narrowly defined scope and definition; affects a single business unit and has a single decision-maker; has access to project information and will not require automated solutions from external project sources; uses the project manager as the primary source for leadership and decision-making; has no political implications with respect to proceeding or not proceeding; produces straightforward deliverables with few interdependencies among skill areas; and costs less than $75,000 and has available funding.

Sponsor.* The person or group that provides the financial resources, in cash or in kind, for the project.

Stakeholder.* Persons and organizations such as customers, sponsors, performing organizations, and the public, that are actively involved in the project, or whose interests may be positively or negatively affected by execution or completion of the project. They may also exert influence over the project and its deliverables.

Storming Stage. The second stage of the Tuckman Model. During the Storming stage the team is in conflict and team members are forced to address important issues.

Strawman. A temporary document or item that is used as a starting point and is intended to be replaced when more information becomes available.

Team Charter. A document that provides operating guidelines for the project team.

Team Building. A planned process and activities designed to encourage effective working relationships among team members.

Tuckman Model. A model developed by Bruce W. Tuckman that identifies the distinct stages that small groups go through. The first four stages—Forming, Storming, Norming, and Performing—were developed in 1965 and the fifth stage, Adjourning, was added in 1977.

Work Breakdown Structure (WBS).* A deliverable-oriented hierarchical decomposition of the work to be executed by the project team to accomplish the project objectives and create the required deliverables. It organizes and defines the total scope of the project. Each descending level represents an increasingly detailed definition of the project work.

Index